The Historical Development of the Offices according to the Presbyterian Tradition of Scotland

Copyright © 1995 Jurie van Wyk, University of Stellenbosch. All rights reserved.

No part of this publication may be reproduced, stored in a retrieval system or transmitted in any form or by any means, electronic, mechanical, photocopying, recording or otherwise, without prior permission from the publishers.

Published in 2005 by
Kachere Series
P.O. Box 1037, Zomba, Malawi
ISBN 99908-76-14-2 (Kachere Theses no. 7)
[DTh, University of Stellenbosch, 1995]

Outside Africa the Kachere Series is represented by the
African Books Collective, Oxford, abc@africanbookscollective.com
and Michigan State University Press, East Lansing, msupress@msu.edu

Layout: Klaus Fiedler and Olive Goba
Cover Design: Olive Goba

Printed by Lightning Source

The Historical Development of the Offices according to the Presbyterian Tradition of Scotland

Jurgens Johannes van Wyk

Kachere Theses no. 7

Kachere Series
Zomba
2004

Kachere Series
P.O. Box 1037, Zomba Malawi
kachere@globemw.net
www.sndp.org.mw/kachereseries/

This book is part of the Kachere Series, a range of books on religion, culture and society from Malawi. Other Kachere titles related to the Reformed/Presbyterian tradition in Africa are:

Zacharias Ursinus and Caspar Olivetanus, *Katekisma wa Heidelberg/ Heidelberg Catechism*

John McCracken, *Politics and Christianity in Malawi. The Impact of the Livingstonia Mission in the Northern Province*

Andrew C. Ross, *Blantyre Mission and the Making of Modern Malawi*

T. Jack Thompson, *Touching the Heart. Xhosa Missionaries to Malawi 1876 – 1888*

Andrew C. Ross, *The Spirit Dimension in African Christianity. A Pastoral Study among the Tumbuka People of Northern Malawi*

Yesaya Zerenji Mwasi, *Essential and Paramount Reasons for Working Independently*

Margaret Sinclair, *Salt and Light. The Letters of Jack and Mamie Martin in Malawi 1921-28*

Isabel Apawo Phiri, *Women, Presbyterianism and Patriarchy. Religious Experience of Chewa Women in Central Malawi*

Stephan Kauta Msiska, *Golden Buttons. Christianity and Traditional Religion among the Tumbuka*

Kenneth R. Ross, *Gospel Ferment in Malawi: Theological Essays*

The Kachere Series is the publications arm of the Department of Theological and Religion Studies of the University of Malawi.

Series Editors: J.C. Chakanza, F.L. Chingota, Klaus Fiedler, P.A. Kalilombe, Fulata L. Moyo, Martin Ott, Shareef Mohammad

Abbreviations

AGA 1638-1842	Acts of the General Assembly of the Church of Scotland, 1638-1842. The Church Law Society 1843.
BEM	Baptism, Eucharist and Ministry. WCC.
BUK	The Booke of the Universall Kirk of Scotland, one volume edition.
Compendium	A Compendium of the Laws of the Church of Scotland. Part First and Second. Ed. A. Peterkin.
Forbes' Digest	Digest of Rules and Procedure in the Inferior Courts of the Free Church of Scotland. With an Appendix. Third Edition.
Gillespie, *Notes*	Notes of Debates and Proceedings of The Assembly of Divines and Other Commissioners at Westminster.
God's Reign	God's Reign & Our Ministry.
Inst.	Institution of the Christian Religion by John Calvin. Translated by H Beveridge.
Knox's Hist.	John Knox's History of the Reformation in Scotland. Two volumes. Ed. Dickenson William Croft.
Knox's Works	The Works of John Knox; Collected and Edited by David Laing. Six volumes.
Practice FCS	The Practice of the Free Church of Scotland in her Several Courts.
Proceedings FCS	Proceedings of the General Assembly of the Free Church of Scotland.
Proceedings UPC	Proceedings of the Synod of the United Presbyterian Church, 1848-1856.
Report	Reports to the General Assembly of the Church of Scotland, 1931-94.
Rules and Forms UPC	Rules and Forms of the Procedure of the United Presbyterian Church.
WCF	Westminster Confession of Faith

Acknowledgements

ON COMPLETION OF THIS STUDY I WOULD LIKE TO EXPRESS MY SINCERE appreciation to Prof. E Brown for his patience and guidance. It has all along been a great privilege to be his student. Likewise acknowledgement is due to the internal examiner and the external examiner for their valuable and essential share in finalising this work.

Acknowledgement is due to my colleagues and the Board of Justo Mwale Theological College for their constant support and for the opportunity to complete this study. The Office for Mission and Evangelisation of the Dutch Reformed Church in the Orange Free State is thanked for financial assistance towards research in Scotland. A scholarship received from Die NG Kerk Kweekskool Beursfonds is highly appreciated. A word of appreciation is expressed to the personnel of the libraries at the Theological Faculty of the University of Stellenbosch and the New College Library of the University of Edinburgh. A special word of appreciation is expressed for the most gracious assistance received from Mrs. Norma Henderson up to the very end of this study. I am particularly grateful to Harold and Joanne de Jong and Jessie Maritz for correcting the English, though the final responsibility for any remaining deficiencies is mine.

There are people who played an important part in making the completion of this study possible. To my mother, Mr. and Mrs. J Konigkramer, Mr. J Mentz and Mr. A and the late Mrs. I Farrant, I owe much gratitude. To my wife, Isabell, and sons Jurgens and Christiaan, who for long periods of time had to be content with an absent husband and father, with deep respect I dedicate this work to them.

In the words of John G Lorimer (1842a:xvii), I commend this work "to the care and blessing of the great Head of the church, whose honour in the vindication of the office, and thereby the growing efficiency of the Christian church, it is designed to promote."

Contents

Introduction

Chapter 1
The "Face of the Church" Established

1.1	The Scottish Reformers: the church and its offices
1.1.1	Early documents
1.1.2	The First Book of Discipline
1.2	The reformation of the Scottish established church
1.3	The need for further reformation

Chapter 2
The Development of the Presbyterian Offices

2.1	The struggle for authority in the church
2.2	The offices according to the Second Book of Discipline
2.2.1	Ministers
2.2.2	Elders
2.2.3	Deacons
2.3	The Second book of Discipline and Scottish ecclesiology
2.4	Episcopacy versus presbytery

Chapter 3
The Westminster Assembly and the Presbyterian Offices

3.1	The calling of the Westminster Assembly of Divines
3.2	In search of a jure divino polity
3.2.1	The parties
3.2.2	The debates on church officers
3.2.3	The seat of church power
3.3	The Westminster Assembly and Presbyterianism
3.4	Further developments

Chapter 4
The Church as an Established Institution

4.1	The Moderates and the church
4.2	The Evangelicals and the church
4.3	Bannerman, Macpherson and Macphail
4.4	The church in the process of Presbyterian reunion

Chapter 5
The Teaching and Ruling Elders

5.1   The minister
5.2   The eldership: an overview
5.3   The elder: presbyter or layman
5.4   The presbyter and Scottish Presbyterianism

Chapter 6
The Deacon

6.1   An overview
6.2   The place and duty of the deacon
6.3   The revival of the diaconate

Chapter 7
Twentieth Century Ecumenical Conversations and Scottish Presbyterian offices

7.1   Ecumenical conversations and the offices of the church
7.2   The church of Scotland and its ministry

Chapter 8
Conclusion

Bibliography

INTRODUCTION

TRAINED IN SOUTH AFRICA AT A THEOLOGICAL FACULTY WITH A DUTCH BACKground influenced by Scottish ministers, I was called to the office of minister in the Church of Central Africa Presbyterian, Nkhoma Synod, a church brought forth by the church of my training, the Dutch Reformed Church in South Africa. In the missionary phase of this Central African church, the Dutch Reformed Church in South Africa once more encountered the offices of the Scottish presbyterian tradition.

From the beginning it was clear that compared to the Dutch Reformed Church in South Africa a different approach to the ministry is followed. It is a ministry to which I am not a stranger, but in which a different conception is apparent and is maintained. I came to realise that the respective Dutch-South African and Scottish presbyterian traditions of Calvin have points of agreement, and yet at the same time, differ from one another. The difference reveals itself especially in the manner in which the offices of minister, elder and deacon are conceived and function.

In the course of time it became evident that to comprehend the traditions, which took, hold in the Reformed churches of Central Africa one must understand the origin and development of the presbyterian offices. I share the conviction of JM Cronjé, a long-time missionary in the Reformed Church in Zambia, that very little of the South African Dutch Reformed Church's appeal to, and alleged reliance on, an ecclesiology typical of the Netherlands reformed tradition is found in the practice of the churches in Central Africa that resulted from its missionary work.[1]

I believe that exposure to the background and development of the offices in Scotland will assist the reformed and presbyterian[2] churches in

---

[1] Cronje, 1958:99
[2] There are a number of churches in Central Africa referring to themselves as Reformed or Presbyterian. On the one hand, the CCAP Nkhoma Synod, established by mission work of the DRC in South Africa, is viewed by the DRC as reformed. The

Central Africa to develop a more relevant ministry of the offices within their own context. Such development is necessary in the light of the dire felt need for a relevant reformed African ministry with office-bearers in touch with their own people and the situation of our day. Rethinking and reconstructing the offices in a scriptural sense, one must discover the origins of the present unsatisfactory system. The problem is that the present ministry is considered to be Dutch Reformed while in reality it is Scottish Presbyterian.

It is, therefore, proposed that the background of the specific expression of the offices in Central African reformed and presbyterian churches, as well as the problem of an indigenous conception, is found in the origin and the development of the offices in the Scottish Church. The Scottish presbyterian church, starting from Calvin, developed its own indigenous approach and practice of the offices. One becomes aware of a continuing problem with regard to the offices in terms of an incomplete development. Contemporary discussion in the Church of Scotland brings out clearly that it is not merely a matter of contemporary reflection, but the manifestation of an age-old, unsolved problem. Scottish presbyterianism has never really come to terms with episcopacy. On the one hand, there were those who held strongly to the presbyterian ideal, viz., of presbyters governing in terms of the various church courts. On the other hand, there were those who continued to endorse episcopalianism and emphasised the central role of the minister in the government of the church. These differences maintained themselves within the development of a peculiar Scottish concept of the church.

Both episcopalianism and presbyterianism acknowledge the Lordship of Christ over His church. The difference between the two systems is

---

CCAP Nkhoma Synod refers to itself as Presbyterian after the name given to the Church of Central Africa Presbyterian when the two presbyteries of Blantyre (Church of Scotland) and Livingstonia (Free Church of Scotland) united as one church in 1924. They were joined by Nkhoma Synod in 1927 (Pauw, 1981:265ff). On the other hand, the Reformed Church in Zambia which traces its origins to the missionary work of Malawian converts, and was supported by the Dutch Reformed Church in the Orange Free State, maintains a polity similar to that of the CCAP Nkhoma Synod. This church presently assists in training ministers from the Reformed Church in Zimbabwe, the Reformed Church in Botswana, the Presbyterian Church of Southern Africa (Zambia Synod), the CCAP Zambia Synod and the CCAP Livingstonia Synod.

found in the primary premise as to who represents the rule of Christ in the church.

Episcopalianism maintains the rule of Christ through the monarchical rule of one individual - the bishop - in terms of substitute representation. In an episcopal system the bond with Christ is found in an unbroken continuity of ministerial order deriving from the apostles themselves. Transmission of the office is by ordination and laying on of hands by those who stand in the historic episcopate. The conviction is that "the Episcopate symbolizes and secures the apostolic mission and authority within the Church."[3] A threefold hierarchy of offices - bishop, priest and deacon - is by ordination distinguished from the laity as a separate clerical order. The bishop, as the highest office, in his "official capacity represents the universal Church to the local Church, and the local Church to the universal Church."[4] He is "the primary local embodiment of that personal, gracious, loving authority which stems from Christ himself."[5] The bishop is considered "the organ of unity and of universality."[6]

The Scottish reformers, in accordance with the teaching of Calvin, rejected the substitution of the rule of Christ in His church by the individual presbyter. The conviction was that Christ rules in His church through His Word and Spirit. The bond with Christ is through confession of faith. Apostolic succession was understood to be the perpetuation through history of the apostolic faith and witness to Christ.[7] It is, therefore primarily related to Word and sacraments, which are faithfully ministered.[8] The concern was, therefore, to establish the true marks of the church, the preaching of the Word, the administration of the sacraments and the exercise of discipline.[9] The emphasis was on the believers gathered around the Word and sacraments. The reformers distinguished three offices viz., minister, elder and deacon, related to Christ and His church

---

[3] Report, 1966:637
[4] Report, 1966:644
[5] Report, 1966:644
[6] Report, 1966:638
[7] Cameron, 1993:21
[8] Report, 1965:703
[9] Knox's Hist., ii.266

and to serve in His name.[10] With the emphasis on function rather than office, the representation of the rule of Christ in the church is expressed in terms of a relationship rather than a position. All offices are held to be equal and Christ is Lord of all. These important reformed principles were not consistently retained in Scottish reformed ecclesiology.

Tracing their roots to Calvin, the presbyterian and the presbyterial-synodical systems of church government developed differently. The starting-point in the presbyterial-synodical system of church government is the *authority* of Christ providing *offices* through which the *church* is gathered, built and protected.[11] The local congregation is fundamental in this system of church government and is considered complete church expressive of the universal church. It is here that Christ exercises His direct rule through His Word and Spirit, using office-bearers.[12] The office of the presbyter characterises the system.[13] All offices are equal and no office may rule over another office.[14] The wider church connection[15] is expressed in the congregation of the local churches in the presbytery, synod and general synod through their representatives. The decisions of the broader assemblies are binding, but all actions and decisions are

---

[10] cf. *Ordonnances Ecclésiastique* of Geneva (Pont, 1981:21-47); *The Forme and Ministration of the Sacraments, etc, used by the English Congregation at Geneua: and approved by the famouos and godly learned man, John Caluin* (Knox's Works, iv:159-214, 172); Inst., IV.I.10; Milner, 1970:101ff

[11] Spoelstra, 1991:58

[12] Coertzen, 1991a:222

[13] Brown, 1992:703

[14] Pont, 1981:103

[15] It is rather difficult to translate the Dutch word "kerkverband" which gives expression to the understanding of the relation between the local church and the wider church according to the presbyterial-synodical system of church government. The same is true for the word "wider" which is a poor translation of the concept "meerdere". In this system of church government, it is important to note that the wider meetings are not considered as church courts; the presbytery, synod and general synod are not expressive of the unity of the church, and are not considered in terms of courts hierarchically ordered with authority centralised in the highest and general synod.

subject to control by the Word of God.[16] Therefore the authority of Scripture is considered vital.[17]

Scottish reformed ecclesiology - fundamental to church offices - was all along conditioned by a specific ecclesiological and political context. The compromise with episcopacy to facilitate a national reformation and the resolve to resist state control with its preference for the bishop led to the rule of Christ being replaced by a substitute representation in terms of offices in courts hierarchically ordered, with authority centralised in the highest and general assembly. Thus the church as an institution exercising the authority of Christ through office-bearers in assembly became the starting-point in presbyterianism.[18] Scottish reformed ecclesiology shifted from Calvin's emphasis on the authority of Christ and the priority of the offices as the departure point in church government to the visible church as an institution understood in terms of the universal church. The presbytery became fundamental in this system of church government. The offices were relegated to a secondary position in Scottish presbyterian ecclesiology, and became functionaries of the institution. Insufficient attention given to the Calvinistic emphasis on the parity of the reformed offices of minister, elder and deacon led to a consideration of the offices in terms of rank and dignity and to an early conviction that the "greater" includes the "lesser." In this way presbyterianism, as distinct from the presbyterial-synodical system of church government, is an adapted episcopalianism. The consequences of the compromise between episcopacy and presbytery are reflected in the Scottish presbyterian consideration of the reformed offices. In the course of presbyterian ecclesiological reflection the sixteenth and seventeenth century emphasis on Scripture and confession to determine the presbyterian viewpoint was replaced by an emphasis on traditional historical associations in the context of twentieth century ecumenical discussions. In effect, however, the development of the reformed offices in presbyterianism is still not finalised.

---

[16] Jonker, 1965:27
[17] Coertzen, 1991a:221-222
[18] Spoelstra, 1991:58

This ambivalent tradition was brought to Central Africa by the various Scottish missionaries, embraced by Dutch Reformed Church missionaries with their own Scottish background, and accepted and maintained by the African church. Considering the history of the Scottish presbyterian offices, the necessity for re-thinking and re-stating the offices in a contemporary context and a reformed sense will become clear.

Major historical definitions and viewpoints reflecting the Church of Scotland's understanding of her ministry in terms of her offices and their institution and function were studied, analysed and evaluated. The following sources were consulted: printed and primary documents related to the various attempts at reforming the Church of Scotland, with special emphasis on those documents that played a formative role in the Church's understanding of the official ministry; published works describing or presenting the definition and function of its offices, including published records by the church itself, e.g. reports to and minutes of assemblies; and pertinent articles from periodicals.

A revealing and typical difficulty in dealing with the history of the Church of Scotland is the partisan nature of much of the material presented by Scottish writers. Writers committed to an episcopal form of church government have a different emphasis from those favouring a presbyterian orientation. In the same way a writer from a later secessionist church has a different emphasis from one from the Church of Scotland, in spite of the fact that both are presbyterian. A modern revisionist approach, although very helpful in assisting the newcomer to Scottish church history to proceed far more cautiously in this maze of fact and interpretation, does not avoid subjective preferences.

In dealing with the "Scottish church" reference is made to the official Church of Scotland as well as to those churches that seceded from it and to the united connections. The literature on the offices of the church represents authors from the various Scottish presbyterian traditions, which consider themselves as continuing the traditional or national Church of Scotland. Works on the church and its offices are contextually conditioned by a specific time and a specific school of thought. For example, it was observed that the strong appeal to Scripture and the conviction of a *jure divino* polity characteristic of the mid-seventeenth century had, by the latter part of the twentieth century, made way for a much more ecumenically orientated and pragmatical approach in determining the function and place of the offices in the church.

During the mid-seventeenth century ecclesiastical controversy, the offices of the Church of Scotland received attention mainly as part of wider works on the order and government of the church, works reflecting the classical expression of presbyterianism.[19] Arising from a Scottish evangelical background, comprehensive works on the church, including discussions on its ministry, were published during the second half of the nineteenth century and early twentieth century. Reference is made to the elaborate work of James Bannerman, a pre-Disruption evangelical, and from 1849, professor at the Free Church New College, Edinburgh. His son published his lectures as *The Church of Christ: Treatise on the Nature, Powers, Ordinances, Discipline, and Government of the Christian Church,* in two volumes in 1868. It has been republished three times during recent decades.[20] Standard works from an evangelical perspective and representing a more pragmatic approach to the ministry of the church were published by John Macpherson, minister of the Free Church of Scotland. His first book, *Presbyterianism Handbook for Bible*

---

[19] cf. Baillie, Robert, 1645, *A Dissuasive from the Errours of the Time: Wherein the Tenets of the Principal Sects, especially the Indepedents, are drawn together in one Map, for the most part, in the words of their own Authours, and their maine principles are examined by the Touch-Stone of the Holy Scriptures*; Baillie, Robert 1646, *An Historical Vindication of the Government of the Church of Scotland*; Gillespie, George 1641, *An Assertion of the Government of the Church of Scotland in the Points of Ruling Elders, and of the Authority of Presbyters and Synods*; [Gillespie, George] 1647, *A Form of Church Government and Ordination of Ministers contained in CXI Propositions propounded to the late General Assembly at Edinburgh*; [Henderson, Alexander 1641], *The Government and Order of the Church of Scotland*; Henderson, Alexander 1644, *Reformation of Church-Government in Scotland, cleered from some mistakes and Prejudices, by the Commissioners of the General Assembly of the Church of Scotland now [The Westminster Assembly] at London*; Rutherford, Samuel 1644, *The Due Right of Presbyteries or, A peacable Plea for the Government of the Church of Scotland*; Rutherford, Samuel 1646, *The Divine Right of Church-Government and Excommunication: or A Peacable Dispute for the perfection of the holy Scripture in point of ceremonies and Church Government in which the Removal of the Service-Book is justified*.

[20] Cameron, 1993:56

Classes and Private Students, was published in approximately 1883,[21] and the second, titled *The Doctrine of the Church in Scottish Theology*, was first published in 1903. In writings from representatives of the Scoto-Catholic movement[22] in the late nineteenth century Church of Scotland, attention was given to the subject of the ministry of the church. Concerned about the recovery of the catholic tradition in the Church of Scotland and enthusiastic about ecumenism, they maintained the necessity of a proper ordination, a valid ministry, apostolic succession, a twofold order of bishop or presbyter and deacon, and the necessity of liturgical improvements.[23] They were followed, in the twentieth century, by James Cooper who was strongly inclined towards Anglicanism.[24] The theological principles of this movement were set out in *A Manual of Church Doctrine* by HJ Wotherspoon and JM Kirkpatrick [1920] (second edition revised and enlarged by TF Torrance and RS Wright in 1960). Alexander Wright (1895) held a high view of the ministry but he had objections to the approach of the Scoto-Catholics.[25] GMS Walker[26]

---

[21] An eighth edition was published in 1949 (Van 't Spijker, 1990:327, footnote 2).

[22] Cameron, 1993:756, 790

[23] cf. Sprott, GW 1873, *A Valid Ordination Essential to the Christian Ministry, and the Exclusive Right of Presbyteries to Ordain: A Sermon preached at the opening of the Synod of Aberdeen, 8 April 1873*, reprinted June 1896; Sprott, GW 1877, *The Church Principles of the Reformation. A Sermon preached before the Synod of Lothian and Tweeddale*; Sprott, GW 1895, "Neglected Provisions and Remediable Defects in the Presbyterian Organisation, and its better adoption to existing needs," in *Scottish Church Society Conferences, Second Series: Vol. II: The Divine Life in the Church. An Affirmation of the Doctrine of Baptism with contributions relating to The Scottish Church, her History, Work, and Present need*, 59-66; Sprott, GW 1882, *Worship and Offices of the Church of Scotland*; Milligan, William 1893, *Scottish Church Society, Some Account of its Aims*; Wotherspoon, HJ 1909, "Adequate Security for the Continuance of the Ministry," in *Re-Union: The Necessary Requirements of the Church of Scotland. Scottish Church Society Conferences. Fourth Series*; Scottish Church Society 1929, *Presbyterian Orders. Occasional Papers IV* first printed 1926; Story, RH 1897, *The Apostolic Ministry in the Scottish Church*.

[24] Cameron, 1993:211

[25] Wright, Alexander 1895, *The Presbyterian Church. Its Worship, Functions, and Ministerial Orders*.

[26] Walker, GMS 1955, "Scottish Ministerial Orders," in *Scottish Journal of Theology*, 8.238-254.

(1955) concerned himself with a synthesis between episcopacy and presbyterianism. The most comprehensive work on the subject of ministerial orders in the first two centuries after the reformation is that of JL Ainslee (1940), *The Doctrine of Ministerial Order in the Reformed Churches of the 16th and 17th Centuries*. GD Henderson presented a non-controversial and traditional presbyterian approach in the Baird Lectures of 1951, published as *Church and Ministry: A Study in the Scottish Experience*. JKS Reid struggled with the question of a biblical doctrine of the ministry.[27] Stewart Mechie[28] (1963) concerned himself more formally with the historical development of the education of ministers in the Church of Scotland, and Duncan Shaw[29] (1969) dealt with the question of ordination of ministers in the early reforming Church of Scotland.

The elder, being a more controversial office, received ample attention. A work ascribed to James Guthrie of Stirling, *A Treatise of Ruling Elders and Deacons*, was first published in 1652. It was revised and republished by order of the General Assembly of 1690. Less controversial than other works of this period, this work concentrated on advice for the improvement of the office of the elder and became characteristic of most of the later works on the subject. From the side of the Evangelical party in the pre-Disruption church[30] and the United Secession Church, a number of works appeared in the early 1840s.[31] From this quarter, the elder as presbyter with appeal to 1 Tim 5:17 was maintained. Taking a

---

[27] Reid, JKS 1955, "The Biblical Doctrine of the Ministry," in *Scottish Journal of Theology Occasional Papers*, 4:1-47.

[28] Mechie, Stewart 1963a, "Education for the Ministry in Scotland since the Reformation," in *Records of the Scottish Church History Society,* xiv.115-133; Mechie, Stewart 1963b. "Education for the Ministry in Scotland since the Reformation," in *Records of the Scottish Church History Society,* xiv:161-178.

[29] Shaw, Duncan 1969, "The Inauguration of Ministers in Scotland," in *Records of the Scottish Church History Society,* xvi:35-62.

[30] *The Presbyterian Review and Religious Journal, November 1834-May 1935,* VI.28-44; 161-177; Lorimer, JG 1842, *The Eldership of the Church of Scotland,* first published in 1841.

[31] King, David 1844, *The Ruling Eldership of the Christian Church*; M'Kerrow, J 1846, *The Office of the Ruling Elder in the Christian Church: Its Divine Authority, Duties and Responsibilities.* Dickson, David 1871, *The Elder and His Work.*

position not far from episcopalians, Peter Colin Campbell, then principal of Glasgow University, strongly opposed any idea of the elder being a presbyter and argued for its lay character, since the office was representative of the people.[32] His viewpoint was taken up in the twentieth century, especially by those committed to ecumenical discussions in which the Anglican Communion featured strongly.[33] William Mair[34] concerned himself with the elder's position with regard to subscription to the standards of the Church of Scotland. The issue of women in the eldership received attention in the early 1930s.[35] In 1935 GD Henderson published the major work, *The Scottish Ruling Elder*. A concern for the effective functioning of this office has been addressed since the late 1950s.[36] Training for the eldership received attention especially after 1960.[37] In the heat of the discussion on the status of the elder in the late 1980s, Peter Donald presented the enlightening dissertation, *'Anent the ministry of the eldership': An aspect of reformation in the Church of Scotland*, towards the degree of B.D. Honours at New College, University of Edinburgh, in 1990.

The reformed office of the deacon has received scant attention. It was discussed only in single chapters in books dealing with the eldership and

---

[32] Campbell, PC 1866, *The Theory of the Ruling Eldership or the Position of the Lay Ruler in the Reformed Church Examined*.

[33] Cooper, James 1907, *The Elder: The Nature of his office, and his opportunities of usefulness in the present day*. An address delivered to the Church of Scotland Officebearers' Association of the Presbytery of Dundee; Balfour Paul, Sir James 1912, "The Post-Reformation Elder," in *Scottish Historical Review*, ix.253-262. Barbour, GF [1934], *The Elder and His Work*. Prepared at the request of The Central Council of the Church of Scotland Elders' and Officebearers' Union; Torrance, TF 1984, "The Eldership in the Reformed Church," in *Scottish Journal of Theology*, 37:503-518.

[34] Mair, William 1880, *The Elders' Formula in the Church of Scotland*. A Letter to the Right Honourable Lord Polwarth.

[35] Henderson, GD, n.d., *Women in Eldership*.

[36] Wilkie, George D 1961, *The Eldership Today*, first published in 1958; MacDonald WC 1958, *The Elder His Character and His Duties*; Anderson, DF 1969, *The Elder in the Church Today*.

[37] *A Course for Elders* 1963-1964, 2 Volumes, Commission on Adult Education; Matthew, S and K. Scott 1986, *Leading God's People*; Matthew, Steward and Ken Lawson 1989, *Caring for God's People. A Handbook for Elders and Ministers on Pastoral Care*.

called for the revival of the office.[38] The only book published on the post-reformation deacon was that of Lorimer in 1842, *The Deaconship. A Treatise on the Office of the Deacon with suggestions for its Revival.* GD Henderson (1935) gave an overview of the history of the office of the deacon in a chapter titled "The Elder at the Plate."

From this brief overview of major works on the offices in the Scottish presbyterian church it appears that there is need for a comprehensive historical and theological study on the Presbyterian offices.

The following outline is used to present the research on the topic concerned.

In chapter one attention is given to contemporary documents expressing the views of the Scottish reformers on the ministry in the local congregation. The Scottish reformers, however, had to come to terms with the reformation of the undivided, established and episcopal Church of Scotland after the success of the military operations of 1559 and 1560. Both the reformers' concern for the ministry in the local congregation and the reformation of a national church had to be dealt with. These issues received attention in the *First Book of Discipline.* Convinced that Scripture supported Calvin's model of church government, the Scottish reformers did not enter into a renewed scriptural justification of their reformation programme. The adaptation of Calvin's model, devised for a single city, was conditioned by the typical Scottish political and ecclesiastical context and a typical Scottish "common sense" approach followed by the reformers in dealing with problems. Episcopal elements were adapted to deal with issues, and the continued involvement of the "godly prince" in the reformation of the church was considered most appropriate. The initial concern for the local congregation was overshadowed by a concern for the church as an overall institution. The starting point in a typical Scottish ecclesiology came to be the church as visible institution representing the universal church. The adaptation of certain episcopal elements, e.g., individual overseers, to serve the reformation plan did not satisfy, while others were retained.

---

[38] Lorimer, JG 1842a, *The Eldership of the Church of Scotland,* first published in 1841; King, David 1844, *The Ruling Eldership of the Christian Church;* M'Kerrow, J 1846, *The Office of the Ruling Elder in the Christian Church: Its Divine Authority, Duties and Responsibilities;* Dickson, David 1871, *The Elder and His Work.*

The second chapter deals more specifically with the question already present at the beginning of the reformation as to who represents Christ - the bishop or the presbyter? It became necessary to give detailed attention to the government of a national church and to resist domination of the church by the civil authority. Andrew Melville could not accept the reconciliation of the episcopal system with the system Calvin shaped. The choice was between the existing episcopal system with its implied royal control of the church, or the development of a new system in which the parity of ministers could be maintained and the involvement of the state in matters of the church could be excluded. The emphasis on the parity of ministers led to a new stress on the courts. The "particular elderships," that would become the presbytery, was described in the *Second Book of Discipline*. This regional organisation, consisting of presbyters, took the place of the bishop and his diocese. The *Second Book of Discipline* represented a more consistent adaptation of the episcopal system to a scriptural and reformed understanding of the church. In this process the relationship between the local congregation and the offices was affected.

The documents of the Westminster Assembly of Divines determined the future course of Scottish presbyterian ecclesiology. This receives attention in the third chapter. In the struggle for the seat of church power, English Puritans and Scottish Presbyterians had to face Erastianism and Independentism. In reaction to, and in accordance with the *Second Book of Discipline,* form and content were given to a comprehensive presbyterianism - scripturally as well as confessionally defined. The emphasis fell on the church as constituted institution with authority vested in official assemblies. The Westminster Assembly documents confirmed the presbytery as the fundamental unit in the government of the church. With the completion of these documents, the adaptation of episcopacy to the scriptural and reformed conviction of the church was also completed. What remained unresolved in this adaptation was the position and function of the reformed offices.

With the pattern of presbyterianism established, the development of the offices within the context of the established presbyterian church is considered in chapters four to seven. In chapter four attention is given to the emphasis on the church as a constituted institution understood in an episcopal sense, as the dominant feature in Scottish reformed ecclesiology and as vital to the development of the offices. The Church of Scotland in its subordinate documents professed Christ to be the sole Head of the church. However, in practice the, question as to the right of the church to be in control of her own affairs was interpreted in different ways. On the one hand, both the approaches of the Moderates during the eighteenth century and of the Evangelicals during the nineteenth century led to secession. On the other hand, the continued domination of the church as a constituted institution in Scottish reformed ecclesiology was reflected in the processes of presbyterian reunion. The emphasis on the church as institution in terms of the universal church in the continued struggle for the spiritual freedom of the church prevented the unfolding of a reformed theology of the offices.

An overview is given in chapters five and six with reference to the understanding of the place and function of the offices of the minister, elder and deacon in Scottish presbyterianism. The compromise with episcopacy is reflected, on the one hand, in the consideration of lower offices as assistants of the higher offices, which prevented the lower offices - the elder and the deacon - from developing as ministries in their own right. On the other hand, the consequences of the compromise are reflected in the inability of Scottish presbyterianism to arrive at a theology of the offices due to the fact that the ecclesiological starting-point was not the authority of Christ using office-bearers to serve His direct rule in the church through His Word and Spirit.

In chapter seven the involvement of the Church of Scotland in twentieth century ecumenical discussions receives attention. These discussions provided a context in which the emphasis fell on organic unity and the problem centred on how to accommodate the various convictions of the offices. At the same time the Church of Scotland involved itself in a major rethinking of its offices in order to improve the ministry of this Church. Two schools of thought distinguished themselves: those in favour of presbyters governing in terms of various church courts and those inclined to an episcopal approach towards church government. It was a context in which the offices were reflected upon with emphasis on traditional historical associations.

By way of a conclusion, an overview on the results of Scottish reformed ecclesiology on the reformed offices and the need for a continuous consideration of the offices in terms of the rule of Christ in His

Church, expressed in a scriptural and reformed sense, is given in chapter eight.

CHAPTER 1

THE "FACE OF THE CHURCH" ESTABLISHED

Introduction

THE FIRST CONCERN OF THOSE IN SCOTLAND WHO WERE CONVINCED OF THE reformed faith was to regulate the ministry of the local congregation. The influence of Geneva was apparent in the attempt to reform the ministry of the Church of Scotland, but a specifically Scottish interpretation emerged at a very early stage. Three factors influenced the Church of Scotland's understanding and development of its ministry. There was the influence of the reformation on the continent, especially Geneva, the reality of a national episcopal church that needed to be reformed, and the struggle between church and state for the authority of the church.

Before there was "the face of the Church"[1] in Scotland, protestant congregations were formed more or less in secret. It was especially from 1555 that "privy kirks" came into being and the reformed faith spread and was fostered throughout the Lowlands.[2] In this process protestant preachers and protestant nobles cooperated.[3] Their political and military activities eventually contributed to the reformation of the established Church of Scotland.

---

[1] Knox's Works, i.300
[2] Donaldson, 1972:50
[3] Renwick, 1960:64; Calderwood, i.326; Knox's Works, i.373-374; vi.674; Reid, 1974:163

By the end of 1558 the reformers endeavoured to have the "face of a public kirk" through the creation of an authority to exercise discipline. John Knox wrote:

> And this our weak begynnyng God did so bless, that within a few monethis the hartes of many was so strengthened, that we sought to have the face of a Church amonges us, and open crymes to be punished without respect of persone. And for that purpose, by common electioun, was eldaris appointed, to whom the whole brethren promised obedience: for at that tyme we had na public ministeris of the worde.[4]

Elders and deacons were appointed and godly laymen were recognised as preachers of the Word to make up for the lack of ordained ministers.[5]

A reformed church organisation, though still at the congregational level, was active by the end of 1559. Donaldson observed that alongside the crumbling old church system, undermined by secularisation, a new system had arisen.[6] By the end of that year it was possible to detect two ecclesiastical systems in Scotland.

1.1 The Scottish reformers: the church and its offices

1.1.1 Early documents

The Scottish reformers, in accordance with Calvin, concerned themselves with ensuring a vital, active, confessing church with the worship service at its centre. According to Calvin the preaching of the Word, the administration of the sacraments and the exercise of discipline made this church visible in its gathering, and united the believers of a specific locality in faith and love. The conviction was that Christ through His Holy Spirit used office-bearers to gather, protect and maintain His church. According to the leaders of the reformed conviction these office-bearers were the minister, elder and deacon. Related to Christ and His church they were to serve in His name.[7] The emphasis was on the belief that the authority of office-bearers was vested in Christ who gathers His church. These convictions were expressed in early Scottish reformed

---

[4] Knox's Works, i.300
[5] Knox's Works, ii.151; Knox's Hist., ii.277; Donaldson, 1960:49-50
[6] Donaldson, 1960:49-51
[7] Inst. IV.1.10; IV.XI.I

documents concerning the organisation of the newly formed reformed congregations.

The early "privy kirks" in Scotland needed a certain amount of organisation. In those disturbing times the concern was to regulate the ministry of the offices as well as the worship of the reformed congregations. Knox tells us that the "privy kirks" found it expedient to elect preachers and to appoint elders and deacons.[8] The Order of the Election of Elders and Deacons in the privy Kirk of Edinburgh, in the beginning, when as yet there was no public face of a Kirk, nor open Assemblies, but secret and privy Conventions in the Houses or in the Fields,[9] referring to this early period, sheds some light. After the presentation of an historical overview on the reforming church during this period, this document points out that "the hearts of many private persons" were illuminated and they withdrew themselves from participation in the idolatry of the "Papistical Kirk." But because "the Spirit of God will never suffer his own to be idle and void of all religion" they began reading Scriptures in secret in their homes. It was, however, necessary to put themselves in such order, "as if Christ Jesus had plainly triumphed in the midst of them by the power of the Evangel," because "a variety of persons could not be kept in good obedience and honest fame." Therefore, they elected some to

> occupy the supreme place of exhortation and reading, some to be Elders and helpers unto them, for the oversight of the flock: And some to be Deacons for the collection of alms to be distributed to the poor of their own body.[10]

This *Order* was possibly influenced by *The Forme of Prayers and Ministration of the Sacraments, etc, used in the English congregation at Geneua: and approued by the famous and godly learned man, John Caluin,* (1556).[11] In a short commentary on the Apostles' Creed, the "markes" of the true church were stated to be the preaching of the Word, the administration of the sacraments and the exercise of discipline.[12]

---

[8] Donaldson, 1960:49-50
[9] Knox's Hist., ii.277ff
[10] Knox's Hist., ii.277
[11] Knox's Works, iv.159 ff
[12] Knox's Works, iv.172

This was followed by arrangements for the election of ministers, elders and deacons.[13]

According to the *Forme of Prayers* it was the responsibility of the church to see to it that the minister who was chosen "be not founde culpable af an suche fautes which Saincte Paul reprehendeth in a man of that vocation."[14] The minister had to be able to undertake his charge of distributing faithfully and sincerely the Word and sacraments, teaching the flock in public and admonishing them in private, "remembring alwais, that if anythinge perysshe throughe his defaute, the Lord will require it at his hands."[15] As far as the office and duty was concerned, the minister had to remember that the "charge of the Word of God is of greater importaunce then that any man is able to dispence therwith." Following the apostle Paul's advice, he should be esteemed as minister and dispenser of God's mysteries, "not as lordes or rulers" over the flock. The minister's main task was the preaching of the Word and the administration of the sacraments, "so that in consultations, judgementes, elections, and other politicall affairs, his counsel rather than authority, taketh place." A further duty of the minister was to pronounce the sentence agreed by the congregation for excommunicating someone, "to the end that all thinges may be done orderly, and withoute confusion."[16]

In both documents attention was given to the requirements for and the duties of elders and deacons. They had to be "men of good conversation and honest fame."[17]

The office of the elder was to govern with the minister(s),[18] in consulting, admonishing, correcting, and ordering all "thynges appertayning to the state of the congregation." According to the *Forme of Prayers*, the elders differed from the ministers in that they did not preach the Word nor did they administer the sacraments.[19] In the "privy kirk" they were to serve in this office for one year or more. Since they were not considered full-time workers in the church, but were people who also had private

---

[13] Knox's Works, iv.174ff
[14] Knox's Works, iv.174
[15] Knox's Works, iv.174
[16] Knox's Works, iv.174
[17] Knox's Hist., ii.277
[18] Knox's Hist., ii.277; Knox's Works, iv.176
[19] Knox's Works, iv.176

responsibilities, they had to be released after this period and others be "burdened in their room." This was "thought a petition reasonable of the whole kirk."[20]

Deacons had to be men of "good estimation and report, discret, of good conscience, charitable, wyse and finallye adorned with suche vertues as S. Paul requireth in them." Their office consisted of the gathering in of alms and the faithful distribution of the same, "with the consent of the Ministers and Elders." They were also to provide for the sick and "impotent personnes." They had to take care that the "charitie of godlye men be not wasted uppon loytrers and ydle vagabondes."[21]

The *Forme of Prayers* acknowledged a fourth kind of office, namely that of "Teachers and Doctors."[22]

In these regulations the concern was, as stated by the *Order* of Edinburgh, for the small "flock to put themselves in such order, as if Christ Jesus had plainly triumphed in the midst of them by the power of the Evangel."[23] Contrary to episcopal practice, controlled participation by office-bearers and the whole congregation in the election of the office-bearers was allowed.[24] The system employed in the election of office-bearers did not represent that of a "democracy", but at the same time officers could not simply be imposed upon the congregation. The elders and deacons were to serve for at least a year. The principle was: not an eldership or deaconship for life, nor a permanent office-bearer. According to the description of the functions of these two offices, a clear distinction in rank between the eldership and the deaconship does not appear to have been made. Concerning the office of the minister, the election process was considered complete once the elected nominee was "appointed" to that charge by the officiating minister. The only ceremony of appointment was that "after the election, the Minister geveth thanks to God, with request of suche thinges as shalbe necessarie for his office."[25]

---

[20] Knox's Hist., ii.277
[21] Knox's Works, iv.176
[22] Knox's Works, iv.177
[23] Knox's Hist., ii.277
[24] Knox's Hist. ii.279; Knox's Works, iv.175-176
[25] Knox's Works, iv.176

1.1.2 The First Book of Discipline

The need to supply an official polity for the Church of Scotland became evident as political developments contributed to a possibility of reforming the established Scottish church.[26]

On 17th August 1560 the *Confession of Faith*, later also known as the *Scots Confession*, was adopted by the *de facto* Scottish government and a week later put into use.[27] At the same time two other acts were passed which abolished the celebration of Mass and papal authority.[28] The episcopal system of government with its bishops and dioceses was not abolished. The plan for the establishment of a reformed church, drawn up as early as April 1560, underwent a number of revisions during the autumn of 1560[29] and was not passed during this session of Parliament. Knox wrote: "The Parliament dissolved, consultatoun was had how the Kirk mycht be establissed in a good and godly Policy, whiche by the Papistes were altogether defaced."[30] A commission was appointed to "draw in a volume the Polecey and Disciplyn of the Kirk, as weill as thei had done the Doctrine."[31] This commission consisted of John Winram, John Spottiswood, John Willock, John Douglas, John Row, and John Knox. The policy was also discussed during the first "General Assembly" which met from 20th to 27th December 1560 in Edinburgh.[32] The Privy Council, consisting of Chatelherault and a small number of prominent protestant Lords who had governed the country since the July-August meeting of Parliament, summoned the Estates for 15th January 1561. At the meeting of the Estates, the religious cause was "fyrste set forward." A revised *Book of Discipline*, as it was called, was presented to the Lords. Six whole days were spent in examination of the *Discipline*. Although a good many nobles and lairds on January 27th signed a statement accepting the *First Book of Discipline* with certain provisos, the *Discipline* never came to enjoy the same legal status as that of the *Confession of*

---

[26] Reid, 1974:181; Knox's Works, i.297-298
[27] Knox's Works, ii.120f.; Knox's Works, ii.257
[28] Knox's Works, ii.128
[29] Cameron, 1972:8, 19
[30] Knox's Works, ii.128
[31] Knox's Works, ii.128
[32] BUK, 1; Row, 1842:16; Knox's Hist., i.343

Faith,[33] one probable reason being the impossibility of implementing the financial provisions, another being that implementation of the principles of the *Book* would have brought about a virtual social revolution.[34]

In this unsettled situation the reformers had to be content with a limited approval. This did not prevent them from implementing the *First Book of Discipline*. They intended to carry out its proposals in the spring of 1561.

The reformation of the church in Scotland did not lead to the formation of a separate protestant church existing side by side with the episcopal Church of Scotland. The concern was for the establishment of a reformed ministry of the Word and sacraments, the exercise of discipline, and the care of the poor in the local congregations within the existing Church of Scotland. In the *Confession of Faith* adopted by parliament on 17th August 1560, the marks of the "true Kirk of God" were stated. These included the true preaching of the Word of God, the right administration of the sacraments, and ecclesiastical discipline rightly administered.[35] These marks, the *Confession* stated, were not merely a reference to the universal church, but to the particular church as "we confess to have in our cities, towns, and places reformed."[36]

This local aspect of the wider church community had to be provided with a ministry. Even before finalizing the *First Book of Discipline* and presenting it to the Convocation in January 1561, the General Assembly, on 27th December 1560, "appointed the Election of the Minister, Elders and Deacons, to be in the public Kirk, and the Preamonition to be upon the Sunday preceding the day of the election."[37]

---

[33] Cameron, 1972:10, 11
[34] Reid, 1974:206; Reid (1974:206-207) pointed out that the implementation of the provisions of the *Book of Discipline* would, for example, have taken away power from the burgesses and lairds who usually chose ministers and elders. This power would then go to ministers and elders of individual congregations. The possible loss of revenue and the realisation by some adherents of the old system that if the *Book of Discipline* were accepted, Roman Catholicism would never be able to return, probably also played a role in not providing legal status to the *Book of Discipline*.
[35] Knox's Hist., ii.266
[36] Knox's Hist., ii.266
[37] BUK, 3

1.1.2.1 The Minister of the Word and Sacraments

Concerning what made men lawful ministers, the reformers stated that in "their judgement touching the Reformation of Religion"[38] it was

> neither the clipping of their crowns, the crossing of their fingers, nor the blowing of the dumb dogs called the Bishops, neither the laying on of their hands, that maketh them true ministers of Jesus Christ. But the Spirit of God inwardly first moving the hearts to seek Christ's glory and the profit of his Church, and thereafter the nomination of the people, the examination of the learned, and public admission (as before is said), makes men lawful ministers of the Word and sacraments.[39]

Under the Fourth Head of the *First Book of Discipline,* attention was directed to the constructive work of regulating and providing for the "lawful ministry."[40] The first matter of importance in a "Kirk reformed or tending to reformation"[41] was that "none ought to presume either to preach, either yet to minister the sacraments, till that orderly they be called to the same."[42] This ordinary calling consisted of "Election, Examination and Admission."[43]

Since the matter of election of ministers had been abused by the "papist church," the reformers found it necessary to treat it more "largely."[44] The participation of the local congregation in the election of the minister was emphasised. The important principle was that "no man be violently intruded or thrust in upon any Congregation."[45] Strict examination of prospective ministers was required. The fact is that ministers were scarce. The reformers, however, felt that he who cannot "break the bread of life to the fainting and hungry souls" cannot be judged a minister. And he, in whose "mouth God has put no sermon of

---

[38] Knox's Hist., ii.280
[39] Knox's Hist., ii.322; cf. also the *Confession of Faith*, Knox's Hist., ii.269
[40] Knox's Hist., ii.283; Cameron, 1972:17
[41] Knox's Hist., ii.283
[42] Knox's Hist., ii.283
[43] Knox's Hist., ii.283-284
[44] Knox's Hist., ii.284
[45] Knox's Hist., ii.284

exhortation" cannot "rightly administer" the sacraments.[46] After the sermon and exhortation, the only procedure which followed to indicate that the person there present was appointed to serve that church was the public approbation of the people and the declaration "of the chief minister." At this stage the process of election was completed. The reformers' judgement was that although "the Apostles used the imposition of hands, yet seeing the miracle is ceased, the using of the ceremony we judge not necessary."[47] As in the case of the *Forme of Prayer* and the *Order of Election of Elders and Deacons in the privy Kirk of Edinburgh,* the concept of "ordination" or "consecration" was not used.[48] By holding this service, the minister and the congregation had entered into a binding contract.[49] In the absence of ministers, readers were appointed to read the *Common Prayers* and the Scriptures.[50]

The Seventh Head of the *First Book of Discipline, Of Ecclesiastical Discipline,* strongly pointed out that besides all others who are subject to the discipline of the Church, it is especially the life and conversation of the minister "that ought most diligently to be tried."[51] The moral requirements laid down for ministers, as shown in the *First Book of Discipline*, were rigorous.[52] The elders especially were considered responsible "to take heed of the life and manners, diligence and study of their Ministers."[53] In this regard they were responsible for admonishing and correcting him if necessary. And, if "he be worthy of deposition," it was the elders, with the consent of the church and the superintendent,[54] who must depose him.[55] This disciplinary procedure, in which the elders played a major role, was not simply a handing over of the minister to the

---

[46] Knox's Hist., ii.287
[47] Knox's Hist., ii.286
[48] Shaw, 1969:35-36
[49] Cameron, 1972:20
[50] Knox's Hist., ii:287
[51] Knox's Hist., ii.309
[52] Knox's Hist., ii.285
[53] Knox's Hist., ii.310
[54] On the "superintendent" see *1.2 below*
[55] Knox's Hist., ii.310

wilfulness of elders. As in the case of the election, examination and admission, the wider church was involved.

Every "inferior" kirk also had the responsibility, once a year, to send one elder and one deacon to the church of the superintendent to report on "the life, manners, study and diligence" of their minister to "the end that the discretion of some may correct the lenity [sic] of others."[56] The families of the ministers also were to come under the supervision of the church. The *Forme of Prayers* had given prominent expression to the exercise of discipline by the local congregation; this was repeated in the *First Book of Discipline*, and in June 1562 affirmed by the General Assembly.[57]

To address the issue of constantly improving the newly established ministry, the reformers considered it necessary to establish "Exercises."[58] The purpose of these "Exercises' was that the

> Church of God may have a trial of men's knowledge, judgements, graces; and also, that such as somewhat have profited in God's word may from time to time grow to more perfection to serve the Church as necessity shall require.[59]

Elders were also required to attend Exercises.

1.1.2.2 Elders and deacons

The elders and deacons were active in the development of the early congregations. With no uncertainty about their presence in a reformed church, the Eighth Head of the *First Book of Discipline* began with the moral requirements for such offices: "Men of best knowledge in God's word, of cleanest life, men faithful, and most honest conversation that can be found in the Church, must be nominated in election."[60]

The election of elders and deacons was to be held annually, "lest that by long continuance of such officers men presume upon the liberty of the Church." The decision on the exact procedures concerning "the votes and suffrages" was left to each particular congregation. The required

---

[56] Knox's Hist., ii.311
[57] Knox's Works, iv.178; Cameron, 1972:176
[58] This was a weekly meeting paying attention to matters which concerned the neighbouring churches, and provided an opportunity for instruction of its members.
[59] Knox's Hist., ii.315
[60] Knox's Hist., ii.319-320

period of one year service need not to be strictly applied, as long as such a person was appointed yearly "by common and free election."[61] Deacons, the "treasurers," were not, however, to be compelled to receive the office again for the "space of three years."[62] The authors did not think it necessary that elders and deacons should receive any "public stipend" because their services were only for one year and because they were not completely involved with the affairs of the church.[63]

Elders were required by the *First Book of Discipline* to assist the minister in all the public affairs of the church. This included
> judging and decerning causes; in giving admonition to the licentious lives, [and] in having respect to the manners and conversation of all men within their charge. For by the gravity of the Seniors ought the light and unbridled life of the licentious be corrected and bridled.[64]

In June 1562 the General Assembly found it necessary to stress that the minister should require every elder to assist him "in all his lawfull assemblies."[65] The responsibility of the elders with regard to the supervision of the life, study and manners of their minister has already been referred to.

The office of the deacon, according to the *First Book of Discipline,* was to receive the "rents and gather the alms of the Church, to keep and distribute the same, as by the ministry of the Kirk shall be appointed."[66] It is interesting to note that they could also "assist in judgment with the Ministers and Elders."[67] One of the deacons was required to accompany the elder for the annual report at the church of the superintendent on the life, manners, study and diligence of the minister. Deacons were also permitted to read "in the assembly if they be required, and found able thereto."[68] The first reader at the St. Andrews congregation was a

---

[61] Knox's Hist., ii.310
[62] Knox's Hist., ii.310
[63] Knox's Hist., ii.312
[64] Knox's Hist., ii.310
[65] Cameron, 1972:176
[66] Knox's Hist., ii.311
[67] Knox's Hist., ii.311
[68] Knox's Hist., ii.311

deacon.[69] They were also allowed to join the elders in the meetings of the session.[70] Although no reference was made to the care of the sick, it seems that the deacons did play an active role in this regard, besides the administration of the rents and alms. An Act of the fifth General Assembly required each minister to take an elder and deacon with him to the Superintendent's synod "to consult upon the common affairs of their diocies."[71]

Such was the view of the Scottish reformers of the reformed ministry in the local congregation. Strong emphasis was placed on the right of the local congregation to elect its office-bearers to serve the ministry of Christ. The concern was for a living, active confessing church with the worship service at its centre. The intention was that the true marks of the church be revealed around the preaching of the Word, the administration of the sacraments and the exercise of discipline. This was explained under the *Nineth Head* of the *First Book of Discipline*: "These things, we say, be so necessary, that without the same there is no face of the visible Kirk."[72] Guidelines for the arrangement of worship services, administration of sacraments and other arrangements for the furthering of the gospel were given but it was permitted that "every particular Church, by their own consent, appoint their own policy."[73] Knox and his colleagues did not plan the introduction of a *jure divino* polity,[74] but at an early stage in the progress of reformation, attention shifted away from the ministry of the local congregation to the organisation of the national church. The reformers had to come to terms with the reformation of an established and national episcopal church.

---

[69] Cameron, 1972:38-39
[70] Cameron, 1972:38
[71] BUK, 29
[72] Knox's Hist., ii.312
[73] Knox's Hist., ii.312ff
[74] The Scots Confession, in Cap. xx, clearly stated: "Not that we think that one policy and one order in ceremonies can be appointed for all ages, times, and places; for ceremonies (such as men had devised) are but temporal, so may and ought they to be changed, when they rather forster superstition than that they edify the Kirk in using the same" (Knox's Hist., ii:268).

1.2 The reformation of the Scottish established church

Calvin's *Ecclesiastical Ordinances* was devised for a single city. The French *Discipline*, adopted in May 1559, the same month Knox returned to Scotland, presented principles for the organisation of already existing reformed congregations on a national level, existing side by side with the established Catholic Church.[75] In Holland and Zeeland, in early 1571, at Emden, reformed and refugee congregations followed the example of France, and entered into a synodical relationship.[76] Only later did they form part of an established national church. In both cases the church model of Calvin was adapted to the local situation. The nature of the reformation in Scotland was different and once again required an adaptation of Calvin's model. Convinced of the scriptural agreement of Calvin's model the Scottish reformers did not enter into a renewed scriptural justification of their reformation programme. The adaptation of the Genevan example was determined by the Scottish political and ecclesiastical context and a typical Scottish "common sense"[77] approach followed by the Scottish reformers.

The reformers took control of an existing established episcopal church. Reformation principles had to be applied in about a thousand

---

[75] Speelman, 1994:135. Secret bible study groups grew into local congregations since 1555. In May 1559 representatives from seventy illegal congregations came together in Paris, in secret, to establish a national synodical relationship based on unity in doctrine and policy. This was achieved without state participation (Speelman, 1994:125-185).

[76] Speelman, 1994:187-189. In the Dutch context nobody was forced to become members of the reformed church and people had to apply for membership to the church as a "separate group in society" (Speelman, 1994:192. Translation mine).

[77] In a later century Thomas Reid (1710-1796) developed a typical Scottish realistic approach to life into a philosophy, also known as Scottish Common Sense Realism, to refute the scepticism of David Hume, the idealism of Bishop Berkeley, and the revolutionary social theories of the radical French Enlightenment. With its emphasis on "common sense" it argued that "normal people, using responsibly the information provided by their senses, gave humans immediate knowledge about the nature of their own minds" (Noll, 1983:31). "Common sense" was an important characteristic which determined the development of Scottish reformed ecclesiology.

congregations.[78] In practice the reformation started with the institution as universal church. The initiative moved to the General Assembly. It became a process of reformation from the top downwards. No clear view was expressed by the Scottish reformers as to what kind of national organisation the reformed church should have. This made for a realistic approach to deal with problems. The immediate need of the Scottish Church was of a missionary nature, "to erect and plant Churches" and its aim, a "total Reformation of Religion in the whole Realm."[79] An instrument responsible for evangelisation and supervision had to be found. The Scottish reformers opted for a compromise with the episcopal system to serve the reform plan.

The choice was made for superintendents. The regional organisation of the old church and concepts typical of episcopacy were simply taken over and adapted. Bishops were rejected, but episcopacy as such was not. The medieval dioceses were re-organised into more manageable units.[80] The intention was that each "diocese" be provided with a superintendent. In the absence of a sufficient number of superintendents, conforming bishops were used to act as superintendents and to facilitate the reformation and organisation of the reformed church in their dioceses.[81] The medieval conviction of a close relationship between church and state was maintained. The nobles were held responsible for furthering the cause of the reformation. It was expected of the nobles governing the country after the revolution of 1560 to encourage gifted persons to join the ministry of the church and to nominate superintendents in the "chief" town of a "diocese."[82]

These superintendents were to "plant and erect churches, to set order and appoint ministers, to the countries that shall be appointed to their care where none are now."[83] A very demanding schedule was required of them. They were to be preachers, making "no long residence in one place till their churches be planted and provided of Ministers, or at least

---

[78] Henderson, 1954:48; Donaldson, 1960:111; Burleigh (1960:201) refers to 924 parishes in 1580.
[79] Knox's Hist., ii.280; Burleigh, 1960:165
[80] Knox's Hist., ii.292
[81] Cameron, 1972:125; Donaldson, 1987:1ff; 19ff, 53ff
[82] Knox's Hist., ii.293
[83] Knox's Hist., ii.291

Readers." They were required to travel, staying twenty or thirty days in one place, preaching at least three times per week, "till they have passed through their whole bounds."[84] Having completed their evangelising responsibilities, they could return to their principal town where they were allowed to stay for three or four months preaching and edifying the church. Thereafter they were compelled to be on the move again.[85] This wide commission which involved evangelisation, pastoral supervision, discipline, supervision of the care of the poor, education of the youth, administration, and judicial matters was not reduced by the General Assembly of June 1562, which ruled generally that ministers be "subject to their superintendents in careful admonition." It further instructed the superintendents to inspect the libraries of the ministers.[86]

A major responsibility of the superintendents was the examination and admission of ministers to congregations. The Lords, in their partial approvement of the *First Book of Discipline* in January 1561, recommended that
> none be admitted to preach, but they that are qualified therefor, but rather be retained readers; and such as are preachers already, not found qualified therefore by the Superintendent, be placed to be readers.[87]

The June and December General Assemblies of 1562 made explicit regulations for the examination and admission of ministers by superintendents and provided that persons who had not been examined and admitted by the superintendent should be prohibited.[88] Apparently the superintendent could also transfer ministers by his sole authority.[89] Excommunication could not be pronounced without consent from the superintendent. It was arranged in 1565, for instance, that if ministers, exhorters and readers refused to follow the superintendent's admonition, the latter could suspend them from their ministry and stipend until the

---

[84] Knox's Hist., ii.292
[85] Knox's Hist., ii.293
[86] Donaldson, 1960:121
[87] Knox's Hist., ii.288
[88] Donaldson, 1960:122; BUK, 15-16, 27; Calderwood, ii.185-206
[89] Donaldson, 1960:122; Calderwood, ii.208, 281, 191

next General Assembly should decide the matter. But in 1576 this power of the superintendent to suspend was restricted.[90]

In both the *First Book of Discipline* and *The Forme and Order of the Election of Superintendents, which may serve also in the Election of all other Ministers,*[91] the superintendent was subjected to the "censure and correction of the Ministers and elders, not only of his chief town, but also of the whole Province" under his care, and to the "Discipline of the Kirk" as was the rest of his brethren.[92] Ultimately they were subject to the authority of the General Assembly and were not governors of the church.[93]

These superintendents played an important role and by December 1562 were required by the General Assembly to establish synods.[94] In the first decade of the General Assembly's life, "apart from the power of legislation and oversight retained by the Assembly and the strict control which was exercised upon the superintendents, they were the centre of the whole Church organisation."[95] The superintendent thus fulfilled most of the administrative, disciplinary, and judicial functions which "in an episcopal system pertain to bishops and in a presbyterian system to the presbytery."[96] The presbytery, however, was not as yet a known structure.

In Scottish reformed ecclesiology the status and function of the General Assembly served to support the development of the concept of the church as institution. The emphasis of John Knox is clear in his saying "tack from us the fredome of the Assemblies, and tack from us the Evangell; for without Assemblies, how shall good ordour and unitie in doctrine be kept."[97] The General Assembly, having had its alleged first meeting in December 1560, played an important role in the Church of Scotland. It took the initiative in the reformation of the church. In the struggle against king and bishop "it constituted a representative national

---

[90] Macgregor, 1926:100
[91] Knox's Hist., ii.294
[92] Knox's Hist., ii.275
[93] Ainslee, 1940:109
[94] Cameron, 1972:177
[95] Shaw, 1964:75
[96] Donaldson, 1972:57
[97] d'Assonville 1968:87

Parliament in whose proceedings and decisions the opinions and wishes of the people on the most vital of all questions found expression."[98] Already at this early stage, according to Kirk,[99] the emphasis was on

> conciliar government, on collective decisions by kirk sessions, superintendent's court, synod and General Assembly, with the operation of an appellate jurisdiction from the lower to the higher courts,

with General Assembly as the supreme authority. As Cameron pointed out, "a real attempt" was made "to combine two types of ecclesiastical organisations."[100] Donaldson, convinced that the Scottish reformers' intended the establishment of an episcopal system of government, was of the opinion that by the end of the civil war of 1573

> the likelyhood ... was that at no very distant date the two structures, old and new, would merge completely and that the reformed church would be in full possession of the ancient polity with all its benefits and offices.[101]

In this realistic approach to the reformation of the Church of Scotland in which the Holy Spirit was not considered in connection with the direct rule of Christ in terms of the government of the church, the concern to ascertain the direct rule of Christ came more and more to be replaced by substitute representation in terms of the offices in courts hierarchically ordered. In addition, in the *First Book of Discipline*, the offices of elder and deacon were not considered in terms of distinct ministries, but as assistants to the minister. This development represents a subtle break with Calvin. The foundations were laid for the church as institution to become the starting point in Scottish reformed ecclesiology and the offices to be considered in an episcopal sense of the lower offices being assistants to the higher offices. This adaptation of Calvin's premise opened the way for the development of presbyterianism.

---

[98] Macphail, 1908:149
[99] Kirk, 1980:56
[100] Cameron, 1972:53
[101] Donaldson, 1960:183-184

1.3 The need for further reformation

The adaptation of episcopal elements, namely the superintendent, to serve the reformation and organisation of the national church and the desired partnership with the state in the process of reformation did not satisfy.[102] The later presbyterians disliked the superintendents because they infringed on the parity of ministers. The episcopalians dismissed them because they were not consecrated bishops.[103] Above all, the responsibility placed upon the office of the superintendent was too great for one person. The superintendent could neither satisfy the demands of evangelisation and supervision of local congregations nor give satisfactory expression to the organisational unity of the reformed church. Both in theory and in practice the arrangement was unsatisfactory. More thorough attention needed to be given to the organisation of the church on a national level. Two factors influenced further development: the growing emphasis on the reformed conviction of ministerial parity and the determination to maintain the autonomy of the church against the growing threat of domination by the civil authority. The choice was between episcopacy and presbytery. The process of relegating the reformed offices to a secondary concern in Scottish ecclesiology would be confirmed.

---

[102] Macgregor, 1926:63; Donaldson, 1972:57; for an opposite view see Henderson, 1957:50
[103] Donaldson, 1972:57

CHAPTER 2

THE DEVELOPMENT OF THE PRESBYTERIAN OFFICES

Problems of administration and jurisdiction called for a revision of the *First Book of Discipline*. Insufficient provision for the organisation of the church on a national level, the continuation of the episcopate, and royal interest in the government of the church raised the question of supremacy in ecclesiastical affairs and drew attention to ecclesiastical polity. The development of the reformed offices in the Church of Scotland was conditioned by the struggle between king and bishop on the one hand, and people and presbyter on the other. A typical presbyterian ecclesiology was determined by the answer to the questions of who shares the authority of the church and how that authority is secured. Following a scholastic and doctrinal approach based on reformed principles in formulating the church's view on its polity and its relationship to the state, a renewed Scriptural reasoning appears not to have been considered necessary.

2.1 The struggle for authority in the church

The initial arrangement which attempted to reconcile the needs of state and church did not satisfy. A mechanism was necessary for administration and discipline, and for mediation between church and state. At the Leith Convention in January 1572, Regent Morton succeeded in introducing into the church a few bishops, frequently styled "Tulcan bishops,"[1] who would be appointed to bishoprics as they fell

---

[1] The word 'tulcan' refers to a calf's skin stuffed with straw and placed beside a cow to make her give milk (Donaldson, 1972:58). This term was used to reflect the misuse of the church for material benefits.

vacant.[2] The Concordat of Leith, as it came to be known, sought to preserve intact the ecclesiastical estate in parliament, a constitutional matter of great importance, while the church was given access to financial resources.[3] Within the next couple of years it was discovered that both crown and nobility were manipulating the hierarchy to their benefit.[4] Of a more serious nature was Morton's enhancement of royal authority over the church.[5] This attempt at reconciling the need for ecclesiastical self-administration and the claims of the crown proved unsatisfactory for the church. It brought forth the need to sharpen the defence of ecclesiastical independence. The time for "expediency" had passed.

Between 1575 and 1592 the leaders of the Kirk were engaged in remodelling the Church's polity in order to meet the demands on its local and national administration without having to resort to bishops.[6] At the same time they had to defend the autonomy of the Church against the threat of civil domination. The agreement reached at Leith infringed on a number of reformed principles regarding the ministry. These included the rejection of state interference in matters of the church, the rejection of the formal involvement of a minister in civil affairs,[7] the emphasis on ministerial parity which did not allow a minister to rule over fellow ministers,[8] and the rejection of the episcopal practice of the bishop being a minister at large, not attached to a particular congregation. The General Assembly of 1575 stated that a bishop was essentially a pastor

---

[2] Henderson, 1957:51; Donaldson, 1972:58
[3] Burleigh, 1960:197
[4] Macgregor, 1926:100
[5] Burleigh, 1960:197
[6] Macgregor, 1926:64-65. An important issue was the parity of ministers. This concern required the superintendent at his election to acknowledge both the need for "correctioun and admonitioun," and his subjection to "the hailsume discipline of the Kirk," since the calling of God for a ministry in the church "maketh not men tyrants, nor lordis, but appoynteth tharre Servandis, Watchemen and Pastouris of the Flock" (Kirk, 1980:79; Knox's Hist. ii.275). The *First Book of Discipline*'s "difference betwixt preachers at this time," with reference to the superintendents, was a matter of "expediency" (Knox's Hist., ii.291). The matter of bishops was different. As state appointees they did not submit themselves to the authority of the General Assembly.
[7] Row, 1842:47
[8] Kirk, 1980:79

of one congregation. Any supervision a pastor might exercise beyond his own congregation was considered a duty which a church authority had entrusted to him. This was done in addition to his proper work. Thus the Assembly called upon Morton's bishops to regularize their position by each taking upon himself a particular church. This report was again debated and approved during the April 1576 Assembly which insisted that the power of visitation belonged to the church and not to an individual.[9]

Those in opposition to bishops found a leader in 1574 when Andrew Melville, after several years of teaching in Beza's Geneva, returned to Scotland.[10] In April 1575 he attended his first meeting of the General Assembly as principal of Glasgow College. This Assembly revived the subject of ecclesiastical discipline.[11] Under the influence of Andrew Melville and other leading ministers, a much stronger anti-episcopal line developed.[12] The anti-episcopal party could appeal to Theodore Beza of Geneva in support of their convictions. As early as 1572, and again in 1576, Beza warned the Scots

> that 'bishops ordained by men and brought into the church little by little so as to establish government by a few, degenerate into a new popedom,' and urged 'chasing away of the device of men' since that issue had been resolved by Christ who allowed no superiority among his own disciples.[13]

Beza's reply to Lord Glamis in 1576 condemned episcopacy and recommended the system of courts with elected moderators. Lord Glamis, the Scottish chancellor who realised the implication of the insistance on parity for the civil as well as the ecclesiastical constitution, had requested an authoritative ruling on the matter of polity. Beza's reply, which came to

---

[9] Kirk, 1980:79
[10] Burleigh, 1960:197
[11] M'Crie 1856:51
[12] cf. Kirk, 1980:45 and Donaldson, 1960:190, for opposing views on the contribution of Melville to the development of the *Second Book of Discipline*.
[13] Kirk, 1980:81

be known as *De Triplici Episcopatu*, was translated into English and became influential in both Scotland and England.[14]

The General Assembly of April 1576 decided, apparently with some encouragement from the regent, to appoint a strong committee to discuss the policy and proper jurisdiction of the church and to submit draft proposals.[15] By October 1576, the committees "to consult upon the matter of the policie of the Kirk" had presented "their judgement contained formalie in writt to the Assembly."[16] In 1577 the revised constitution was ready to be submitted to the King, and in 1578 *The Second Book of Discipline* was finally approved by the General Assembly.[17]

The *Second Book of Discipline* established the seat of church authority in its three-fold understanding of the word "church".[18] Firstly, the church was understood in the sense of a visible institution embracing all members, both the godly and the ungodly. Secondly, there was the invisible church consisting of the godly and the elect. Lastly, in a much more narrow sense, it could refer to those appointed to spiritual functions within the community of believers. It was explained that the church understood in this last sense was given an ecclesiastical power by God through Jesus Christ. This power was given directly to the office-bearers who were lawfully called to the spiritual function in the church. They were to exercise this power to the comfort and well-being of the whole church.[19] This power, as *potestas ordinis*, reflected the teaching responsibility of the church, and as *potestas jurisdictionis*, reflected the power exercised "conjunctly be mutuall consent of them that beir the office and charge, efter the forme of judgement."[20]

The position of the church in relation to the state received attention. It was stated that the power and polity of the church was different from that of the civil power, though both were from God and were to be rightly used for the advancement of the glory of God, "to have godlie and gud

---

[14] Donaldson, 1960:19; Avis, 1981:123
[15] Burleigh, 1960:198
[16] Kirk, 1980:47
[17] Macgregor, 1926:108; Donaldson, 1972:73
[18] Compendium, Part 1.109
[19] Compendium, Part 1.109
[20] Compendium, Part 1.110

subjects."[21] It was further stated that the church cannot have any other head on earth but Christ. Thus, no angel or man, "of what estait that he ever be," may be called the head of the Church.[22] The authors continued to formulate the differences in function and responsibility between the office-bearers of the church and the civil government.[23] According to them, the ministers and others of the "ecclesiastical estate" were subject to the magistrate in civil matters, and the person of the magistrate was subject to the church in matters spiritual and ecclesiastical. The exercise of both these jurisdictions could not be fulfilled by one person. The civil power was called the power of the sword and the other was called the power of the keys. Each had a specific function in its own field, each had to maintain respect for the different functions and not transgress into the field of the other. The one dealt with matters external; the other with matters spiritual, of the conscience. The means of obtaining their ends were different - the magistrate used the sword; the church used the spiritual sword and spiritual means. Melville gave his own description of the relationship between church and state when he told James VI that

> The rejection of involvement of the state (with its preference for the bishop) in matters of the church and the emphasis on ministerial parity necessitated a stress on courts and councils. This led in practice to the development of a new organ, the presbytery, which would fulfill the functions of the bishops.[24] In the *Second Book of Discipline* four kinds of assemblies were distinguished - "of particular kirks ane or ma, or of a province, or of ane hail nation, or of all and diverse nations professing one Jesus Christ."[25]

Membership to the assemblies was restricted to ministers, doctors (who were elders unless elected to a charge) and elders.[26] The assemblies were to deal with "ecclesiasticall things" only. Visitation was

---

[21] Compendium, Part 1.110
[22] Compendium, Part 1.110
[23] Compendium, Part 1.111-112
[24] Donaldson, 1960:185; 1972:72
[25] Compendium, Part 1.119
[26] Compendium, Part 1.119

the responsibility of a court (not an individual) and the final end of all courts was "first to keip the religion and doctrine in puritie," and "to keip cumeliness and gude ordor in the kirk."[27] The courts were free to make or repeal rules (which must be in agreement with those of higher courts) for the benefit of all the members of the church under their care.[28] They had power to execute discipline and to punish offenders.

The first court described in the *Second Book of Discipline* was described as consisting of members from different congregations and was called the "particular elderschip." It was still far from clear as to what was meant by elderships or presbyteries. Development in thought and practice was still needed.[29] Sessions for each congregation were not considered necessary,[30] but were maintained in practice. It would appear that the "particular elderschips" together with the "exercises" developed into presbyteries.[31] This court had the responsibility of visiting the churches under its care. It had to ensure that the Word was purely preached, the sacraments administered, discipline exercised and ecclesiastical goods well managed.[32] In addition it had to ensure that the decisions of the higher courts were executed. The eldership had the power of excommunication.[33]

One major obstacle to the development of presbyteries was that, according to a statute of 1567, the power of collation to benefices belonged to superintendents and commissioners, while several other acts of parliament and council had given authority in a variety of matters to bishops, superintendents and commissioners.[34] A settlement arrived at by a conference of ministers and counsellors, which met in February 1586, steered a middle way. The existence of presbyteries was accepted and their formation was to proceed systematically; bishops, nominated by the king and admitted by the Assembly, to which they were also

---

[27] Compendium, Part 1.120
[28] Compendium, Part 1.120
[29] cf. Henderson, 1957:51
[30] Compendium, Part 1.120-121, 132; Kirk, 1980:102ff; Dunlop. 1958:170
[31] Kirk, 1980:102ff; Dunlop. 1958:170
[32] Compendium, Part 1.121
[33] Compendium, Part 1.121
[34] Donaldson, 1960:219

answerable for life and doctrine, were to be permanent moderators of the presbytery meetings within their places of residence.[35]

Alongside the bishops, the growth of presbyteries continued. The *Second Book*, however, remained silent on the transfer of the powers of oversight. As late as 1586, special commissioners were still appointed by the General Assembly to "visit" ministers within their presbyteries. In 1590 it was resolved that these were unnecessary where presbyteries had been "well and sufficiently constituted."[36] In 1592 parliament recognised presbyteries.[37] With the "Golden Acts"[38] of 1592, when for the first time official recognition was given to the policy of the *Second Book of Discipline*, statute laws were brought in line with the practice, which had developed over the last couple of years. This was that presbyteries were becoming involved in the admission of ministers and in regional administration in general.[39]

The provincial assemblies had the power to "handle, order, and redress all things ommittit or done amisse in the particular assemblies."[40] And, "generalie thir assemblies have the haill power of the particular elderships whairof they ar collectit."[41] The national assembly, called "the generall eldership of the haill kirk in the realme," consisting only of "ecclesiasticall persons," was instituted to see to it "that all things aither omittit [sic], or done amisse in the provinciall assemblies, may be redressit and handlit."[42]

In establishing a national organisation for the church and maintaining its independence from the state, the church became defined as a distinct institution. The principle laid down by the authors of the *Second Book of Discipline* that it is Christ himself who rules His church through his "Spreit and word"[43] was not done justice to. In defining their view of authority in

---

[35] Donaldson, 1960:216
[36] Henderson, 1957:53
[37] Henderson, 1957:53
[38] Donald, 1990:22
[39] Donaldson, 1960:219
[40] Compendium, Part 1.122
[41] Compendium, Part 1.122
[42] Compendium, Part 1.122
[43] Compendium, Part 1.110, 112

the church, the authors of the *Second Book of Discipline* not only held on to the episcopal hierarchy and merely replaced the single presbyter with presbyters in assemblies, but also replaced the rule of Christ through His Word and Spirit with the rule of man.

2.2   The offices according to the Second Book of Discipline

That the divine right of spiritual government lodges in the office-bearers of the church was stated in the first chapter of the *Second Book of Discipline* and confirmed by the requirement for membership to church assemblies.[44] The substance of the polity of the church over which the office-bearers presided was described as consisting of doctrine (which included the administration of the sacraments), discipline and distribution.[45] From this division, so the writers of the *Second Book of Discipline* maintained, arose a threefold permanent order of ministry in the church, namely the minister or preacher, the elder or governor, and the deacon or distributor.[46] Out of this threefold order emerged four "functiones or offices in the kirk of God, the office of the pastor, minister or bishop; the doctor; the presbyter or eldar; and the deacon."[47] These offices were considered to be permanent and were not to be added to in the true church of God.

The *Second Book of Discipline*, in defining the procedures for admitting persons to ecclesiastical functions and offices, emphasised reformed practice and the prevention of malpractice. This included emphasis on the concept of vocation or divine calling.[48] Without such lawful calling, nobody was allowed to be involved in any ecclesiastical function. A distinction was made between an extraordinary and an ordinary calling.[49] Besides the calling of God and the inward testimony of "a gude conscience," the ordinary calling consisted of the lawful approbation and outward judgement of men, "according to Godis word, and order establishit in his Kirk."[50]

---

[44]   Compendium, Part 1.109-110; 119
[45]   Kirk, 1980:74; Compendium, Part 1.112
[46]   Compendium, Part 1.112
[47]   Compendium, Part 1.113;
[48]   Compendium, Part 1.113; Kirk, 1980:65
[49]   Compendium, Part 1.114
[50]   Compendium, Part 1.114

This ordinary calling had two parts: election and ordination. Election referred to the choice of the most able person or persons for a specific vacant office by the eldership and with the consent of the congregation.[51] In opposition to episcopal practice, it was repeatedly stated that the intrusion of any person into any office of the church contrary to the will of the congregation, or without the participation of the eldership,[52] or without a lawful calling must be strictly avoided.[53] It was also stated that no one was allowed to be elected to the ministry unless a specific flock were assigned to him.[54] Most importantly, the ministers were to reside amongst their flock, "tak the inspection and oversicht of them, every ane in his vocation."[55] In addition, it was stated that anyone who was called by God and who had accepted the charge of the ministry may not leave the ministry.[56]

Among the abuses which the authors of this *Discipline* desired to eradicate were those which touched upon the reformed principles of admittance to the ministry. They required a rejection of "Papistical titles"[57] on the grounds that bishops "ar all ane with the ministers,"[58] and that each minister be assigned to a particular flock.[59] The General Assembly which approved the *Second Book of Discipline* concluded that "no bishop shall be elected and admitted hereafter, before the next General Assembly."[60] The next General Assembly in June 1578 concluded "that the said act shall be extended to all times to come," until the estate of bishops "be root and branch taken away."[61] This matter

---

[51] Compendium, Part 1.114
[52] Compendium, Part 1.114
[53] Compendium, Part 1.116
[54] Compendium, Part 1.115, 116, 129
[55] Compendium, Part 1.115
[56] Compendium, Part 1.116
[57] Compendium, Part 1.127
[58] Compendium, Part 1.128
[59] Compendium, Part 1.129
[60] Donaldson, 1960:203
[61] Row, 1842:63; Burleigh, 1960:201

received attention during the Assemblies of July 1580 and April 1581.[62] One of the charges brought against the Scottish bishops during the General Assembly of 1638 was that, contrary to the "Book of Policie" (the *Second Book of Discipline*), they had been ordaining "at large" and they themselves had not been "tied to particular flockes." [63] It was stated that the bishops were not pastors of pastors, nor pastors of many flocks "and yit without ane certaine flock."[64] It was again emphasised that it was the responsibility of the church to elect persons to ecclesiastical functions. Both the first and the second *Book of Discipline* condemned the imposing of a minister upon a congregation without its consent. This meant that the church required that patronage and the practice of presentation to benefices be abolished.[65] However, it was the norm in the country and thus the practice in the church. The proposal that a congregation should elect its minister was not granted. Presentation was the method employed in supplying congregations with ministers. In practice, the wishes of congregations often appear to have been taken into account,[66] but presentation by the crown and lesser patrons made no reference to congregational rights.[67]

Contrary to the *First Book of Discipline*, the concept of ordination was introduced in the *Second Book of Discipline*. According to the *Second Book*, ordination referred to the separation and sanctification of the person appointed by God and his church after he had been "weill tryit and fund qualifiet." The ceremonies involved in ordination were fasting, earnest prayer and imposition of hands. The *First Book of Discipline* did not consider any ceremony necessary other than the "public approbation of the people, and declaration of the chief minister."[68] Differences of opinion as to whether "the laying on of hands" was necessary existed until the end of the sixteenth century. In 1597 the Assembly ordered "that

---

[62] Although the *Second Book of Discipline* was, in part, ratified in 1592, bishops were done away with within the Church of Scotland only at the end of the seventeenth century.
[63] Ainslee, 1940:145; AGA, 1838:96-97
[64] Compendium, Part 1.129
[65] Compendium, Part 1.133
[66] Foster, 1975:136; Dunlop, 1958:177
[67] Donaldson, 1960:222
[68] Knox's Hist., ii.286

there be uniformity in the ordinatioun of the Ministrie throughout the haill countrey, imposition of hands."[69] Thirty-six years after the formulation of the *First Book of Discipline,* a definite distinction in rank between the minister and the elders appears to have become the norm. The practice of ordination and arrangements for supervision of the minister contributed to this development. Initially, according to the *First Book of Discipline,* ministers were placed under the control and supervision of the kirk session, and in matters of discipline, the kirk session, which consisted of elders and deacons, together with the superintendent and his court, was the responsible body. The *Second Book of Discipline* placed the discipline of ministers under "particular elderships." It was considered the task of these elderships, and later of the presbyteries, to elect and, when necessary, to discipline ministers.

2.2.1 *Ministers*

"Pastors, bishops, or ministers" were defined as those who were appointed to particular congregations where they ruled by the Word of God over those placed in their charge. They were called "pastors" because they fed the flock.[70] Sometimes they were called "episcopi" because they watched over their flock.[71] Other times they were called "ministers" because of their service and office. Sometimes they were also called presbyters or seniors "for the gravity in manner" which they ought to have in taking care of the spiritual government which "aucht to be most deir unto them."[72]

The task of the minister included the preaching of the Word and the administration of the sacraments. The *Second Book* considered it the responsibility of the pastor to pray for and to supervise the behaviour of those under his care. Disciplinary action also belonged to the pastor, but in co-operation with the eldership. After lawful proceedings by the eldership, the pastor announced the sentence of "binding and lowsing upon any person, according unto the power of the keyes grantit unto the

---

[69] Foster, 1975:144
[70] Compendium, Part 1.115
[71] Compendium, Part 1.115
[72] Compendium, Part 1.115

kirk." The pastor was also made responsible for the solemnisation of marriages.[73]

2.2.2 Elders

The office of the elder clearly justified itself. It was maintained throughout episcopal and presbyterian periods in the national church[74] despite those who wished to know little or nothing of it. The difficulty of balancing civil and ecclesiastical claims was not a minor issue.[75]

The office of the elder did not agree with the Erastian views of James VI.[76] Elders from the presbyteries were not invited to those meetings of the General Assembly, which were arranged especially to suit the king's purposes, as at Linlithgow 1608, Glasgow 1610, Aberdeen 1616 and Perth 1618.[77] His son, Charles I, also appears to have been wholly disinclined to allow a "lay" element to attend church assemblies.[78]

According to the *Second Book of Discipline*, the word "Eldar" in Scriptures refers to age and sometimes to office. When it refers to office, it sometimes includes pastors and doctors as well as those called seniors or elders.[79] Elders are those whom the apostles called presidents or governors. Their office was permanent and always necessary in the church. Furthermore, the eldership was a spiritual function, "as is the ministrie." A new development and without precedent in reformed churches was that elders, once they were lawfully called, could not leave that office again.[80] It was, however, permitted that "ane pairt of them may reliefe anuther for a reasonable space."[81] Another innovation was that the authors were convinced that both elders and deacons should be

---

[73] Compendium, Part 1.116-117
[74] Henderson, 1935:38
[75] Donald, 1990:10, 24
[76] After he increased his power through the union of the crowns of Scotland and England in 1603, his sentiment was simply "Presbytery agrees as well with Monarchy as God and devil" (Ainslee, 1940:16; cf. also Simpson, 1983:27-41).
[77] Henderson, 1935:161
[78] Donald, 1990:24
[79] Compendium, Part 1 118
[80] Compendium, Part 1.118; Donald, 1990:19
[81] Compendium, Part 1.118

paid officials of the church.[82] Not all elders needed to be teachers of the word. Ordination of elders appears to have been required.

It is clear that in defining this office, a much "higher" view of the elder was maintained by the *Second Book of Discipline* than by the *First Book of Discipline*.[83] The divine right of the spiritual government lodged in the offices of the church, including the office of the elder, is stated already in the first chapter of the *Second Book*.[84] In addition, the requirement of an office for life and the desire to change elders into paid officials of the church distinguished them as a seperate clerical class. However, in comparison with the responsibilities assigned to the elders by the *First Book of Discipline* in the matter of the discipline of ministers, their authority was in practice curbed. The *Second Book of Discipline* stated "that to take away all occasion of tyrannie," all officers should rule with the mutual consent of the brethren, and "equality of power, every one according to thair functions."[85] Yet the General Assembly of 1597 agreed that only pastors and doctors were permitted to vote in matters of doctrine.[86]

In substance the elder's task was described thus: "As pastors and Doctors sould be diligently in teiching and sawing the seid of the word, so the elders sould be cairfull in seiking the fruit of the same in the people."[87] Part of the task of the elder was to assist the minister in the examination of those who come to the Lord's table.[88] The General

---

[82] Compendium, Part 1.125
[83] Claims had been made, based on the definition of the *Second Book of Discipline*, that the elder ceased to be a layman, and that he received *indelible character* (Donaldson, 1960:186). Counter claims insisted that "neither in theory nor in practice is there sufficient evidence to confirm the view that the elders of the *Second Book of Discipline* received *indelible character*" (Kirk, 1980: 93).
[84] Compendium, Part 1.109
[85] Compendium, Part 1.112-113
[86] Donald, 1990:18
[87] Compendium, Part 1.119
[88] Compendium, Part 1.119. It appears that from an early stage the elder also assisted at the communion table, though this practice did not receive support from either books of discipline. It was only in 1931 that an official utterance was made by the General Assembly of the United Church of Scotland that "the elders assist the

Assembly of 1563 mentioned the elder's responsibility regarding the visitation of the sick. This function was taken up by the *Second Book of Discipline*.[89] According to Alexander Henderson, the elder was also responsible for catechising the people[90] and examining children in religious knowledge.[91] This was different from his French counterpart who apparently was not allowed (1559) to catechise in public.[92]

Since attendance at the various assemblies was included in their calling, the elders were responsible for the enforcement of the acts.[93] Lastly, they were to hold assemblies with the ministers and doctors to establish "gude ordor, and execution of discipline." All persons within their bounds were subject to the decisions of these assemblies.[94] Elders, however, were generally absent as regular members from presbytery meetings before 1638, though during the early years they might have attended or were at least expected to attend.[95]

2.2.3 Deacons

Through their service and ministery, all who bear office and function in the church were considered by the *Second Book of Discipline* to be "deacons." This was the wider understanding of the word *diakonos* according to the *Second Book*.[96] In the narrow sense of the word, the deacon proper was defined as a financial officer - those "unto whom the collection and distibution of the almes of the faithfull and ecclesiastical gudes does belong."[97] The care of the poor was a special responsibility.[98] As financial officer, the deacon was considered a permanent "ecclesiastical function" in the church, and like the other

---

ministers in the distribution of the elements at the Lord's Supper" (Kirk, 1980:98-99; Henderson, 1641:23; Henderson, 1935:42).
[89] Compendium, Part 1.119
[90] Henderson, 1641:30
[91] Macgregor, 1926:91
[92] Macgregor, 1926:91
[93] Compendium, Part 1.119
[94] Compendium, Part 1.119
[95] Donald, 1990:25; Foster, 1966:23
[96] Compendium, Part 1.123
[97] Compendium, Part 1.123
[98] Compendium, Part 1.124

offices, not a function under the civil power.[99] Their duties had to be fulfilled "according to the judgement and appoyntment of the Presbyteries or elderschips"[100] - to which they did not belong.

Here a modification took place concerning the deacon's position in church courts, as compared to the *First Book of Discipline* which allowed deacons to "assist with ministers and Elders", a practice of which Beza approved in his letter of 1576.[101] According to a strict definition of function, deacons were no longer allowed a place in "presbyteries or elderschips."[102] Despite this loss of the deacon's right of membership and the official narrowing of the popular basis of Knox's church courts, it appears that during the period up to 1638, kirk sessions continued to include deacons.[103]

In practice the deacons never acquired the comprehensive control over church property envisaged by both the first and the second *Book of Discipline.* Their duty, at most, was to collect and distribute funds to the poor.[104] They apparently continued to serve alongside the elders in various leadership tasks.[105] This included communion duties and visitation of the sick, even though neither *Book of Discipline* made provision for these functions.[106] The office of the deacon was frequently neglected or confused with the responsibilities of the elder. It was the practice in some of the parishes to have a deacon for every elder's district, but frequently the number of deacons was much smaller. In some parishes some elders were set apart to act as deacons, while it was reported that at Mauchlin, it was the custom to ordain men as both *elder* and *deacon.*[107]

---

[99] Compendium, Part 1.124; Henderson, 1954:82
[100] Compendium, Part 1.124
[101] Kirk, 1980:98
[102] Compendium, Part 1.119
[103] Macgregor, 1926:124; Dunlop, 1958:175; Kirk, 1980:98; Henderson, 1935:6; Henderson, 1641:31
[104] Kirk, 1980:98; Donaldson, 1960:222
[105] Donald, 1990:25
[106] Henderson, 1954:82; Dunlop, 1958:176; Kirk, 1980:98
[107] Henderson, 1935:70

2.3 The Second Book of Discipline and Scottish ecclesiology

To John Knox the establishment of the "face" of the church was the introduction of office-bearers with their different functions to regulate the worship and ministry in the local congregation. To the *Second Book of Discipline* the "face" of the church was found in the answer to the questions of who shares the authority of the church and how that authority is secured.

Melville could not accept the reconciliation of the episcopal system with the system Calvin shaped. Ministerial parity was a necessary requirement in the reformed church. The bishop could not continue operating as superintendent. Besides, bishops made for royal control of the church. In order to maintain the rule of Christ over the church in the face of royal claims and in order to resist resorting to the presbyter in episcopacy, the *Second Book of Discipline* opted for government by presbyters in assembly with authority hierarchically ordered. This resulted in the development of a characteristically Scottish ecclesiology.

The district eldership that would become the presbytery was adopted and outlined. This regional organisation consisting of elders and ministers took the place of the bishop and his diocese. However, it started with the church as institution representing the universal church. Through the presbytery, the diocese of the episcopal system could be integrated into the reformed church, the authority of the presbyter in episcopacy resisted, the parity of ministers maintained, and the participation of the people in the government of the church (and a voice against royal encroachment) ensured. At the same time, the unity of the church could be maintained by a fellowship of courts graded from lower to higher, with authority hierarchically ordered. The way was opened to consider the courts as expressive of the church as institution. Finally, the episcopal transfer of the government of Christ to man through the single presbyter was maintained - as government by presbyters in assembly.

It was especially the offices in their relation to one another and to the congregation that was affected. In the formulation of the "eldership" the way was opened for the local congregation to be deprived of its character as the autonomous and complete revelation of the universal church, and of its role in the government of the church. Calvin's view of the congregation with the offices strongly tied to it was distorted.[108]

---

[108] Inst. IV.1.10; IV.XI.1

According to Calderwood, writing in the 1620s, the kirk-session was simply a committee of the presbytery.[109] On the one hand, the offices as a separate clerical order with inherent spiritual power to govern was established. On the other hand, a distinction in rank and diginity was made between them - parity of the minister, elder end deacon was not held onto. Only the minister and the elder were considered members of the church courts. The deacon was excluded. The minister was distinguished from the other offices by his ordination. Like the bishop, the minister was given a prominent place in the regional organisation and was no longer subject to the supervision of the local elders and congregation. Despite the "high" view of this *Book of Discipline* on the office of the elder expressed as "a spirituall function, as is the ministrie," who was ordained for life and considered to be a paid official of the church, the responsibilities of the office were curbed. The elder was, in fact, viewed in terms of an assistant to the minister. This approach to the eldership, would prevent its development as a ministry in its own right and it would be considered nothing more than a representative of the people. The deacon, although considered fulfilling a "perpetuall ecclesiasticall function," was restricted to managing ecclesiastical goods, and was in essence an assistant to the elder. In effect, both elders and deacons were reduced to the status of officials of a religious organisation.

With this major rethinking of the polity of the church, the foundations of Scottish presbyterianism were laid. With the *Second Book of Discipline*, a more complete compromise with episcopacy was established. The pattern for future development was provided. With the Westminster Assembly of Divines, it would be Scripturally and confessionally confirmed.

2.4 Episcopacy versus presbytery

The *Second Book of Discipline* was at first not ratified by the government, which declined to recognise ecclesiastical independence.[110] Yet the General Assembly of 1581 enacted that the

---

[109] Burleigh, 1949:295
[110] Donaldson, 1972:73

Second Book of Discipline be registered amongst the Acts of the General Assembly.[111] The government, in turn, defined its standpoint in the so-called "Black Acts" of 1584. These acts asserted the supremacy of the king in church matters and turned the bishops into crown commissioners for the administration of the church.[112] One of the "Black Acts" of May 1584 was aimed at "that form lately invented in the land, called the presbytery, which usurped all the whole ecclesiastical jurisdiction."[113] At this point the difference between state and presbytery became more clearly defined. On the one hand there was the supremacy of the crown and parliament together with the episcopal office in the affairs of the church; on the other hand there was the rule of the General Assembly and ministerial parity.[114] It was an ecclesiological as well as a political struggle. "Hence Melville's determination to ensure that the power continues to lie with the assemblies of the church, which Morton threatened to subvert."[115]

In 1596 James VI felt free to exclude the attendance of elders from presbyteries.[116] It was especially in 1597 that he began his reaction against what was at times called Melvillian presbyterianism[117] which had been established by an Act of Parliament in 1592.[118] From 1612 to 1637 royal policy emphasised the difficult task of moulding Scottish worship into closer semblance of Anglican forms.[119] By 1618 James sought to enforce, by the Five Articles of Perth, such Anglican practices as kneeling at communion, episcopal confirmation, the observance of

---

[111] Brown, 1891:60; Henderson, 1962:145
[112] Donaldson. 1972:73
[113] Donaldson, 1960:211
[114] Donaldson, 1972:73
[115] Kirk, 1980:42, 56. According to Shaw (1964:17) the composition of the assemblies shows that the medieval concept of the church and state as two sides of the same coin made the General Assembly not merely a church gathering but a national council.
[116] Donald, 1990:22
[117] The word "Presbyterian" was not applied to the system preferred by Melville, until the middle of the 17th century controversy on church government in Scotland and England (cf. Burleigh, 1949:293-294).
[118] Dunlop, 1958:161
[119] Dunlop, 1958:158

certain festivals, and private baptism and communion.[120] The changes were relatively small. However, they challenged the reformed pattern of worship established by Knox and the early reformers. Widespread disobedience to the new regulations occurred.[121]

Charles I, the son of James, acceded to the throne in 1625. His attempts, in 1637, at imposing a new liturgy on the Scottish church resulted in strong Scottish resistance. In 1636, the *Book of Common Order*, or Knox's Liturgy, was abolished and the use of "Laud's Liturgy", or the *Book of Common Prayer*, and the Canons and Constitutions Ecclesiastical was enforced; extemporaneous prayer was prohibited, the eldership and presbyterian courts were tacitly abolished, and excommunication was enacted for any denial of royal supremacy over the Scottish church.[122] The day set aside for the introduction of the new service book, 23 July 1637, in St. Giles' Cathedral in Edinburgh, resulted in a riot.[123] The resistance soon became organised. Nobility, lairds, burgesses and churchmen formed a powerful committee, called the Tables, to deal with the issues at hand.[124]

Charles' first abortive attempt at dealing with the resistance resulted in a withdrawal of the Canons and the Liturgy, the summons of a free General Assembly, and the holding of a free parliament.[125]

The General Assembly met in November 1638 in Glasgow. It annulled the Acts of the Assemblies of 1606, 1608, 1610, 1616, 1617, and 1618 as "unfree and unlawful," and gave specific reasons for each annulment.[126] When it became clear that the Assembly was bent on nothing short of abolishing episcopacy itself, the king's commissioner, who also objected to the presence of elders,[127] dissolved it in the name of the king and published a proclamation declaring its continuance

---

[120] McEwen, 1982:8; Burleigh, 1960:208
[121] McEwen, 1982:8
[122] McEwen, 1982:9
[123] McEwen, 1982:10; Burleigh, 1960:217
[124] Burleigh, 1960:217
[125] Burleigh, 1960:219
[126] Dunlop, 1958:165
[127] Henderson, 1935:161

treasonable.[128] The Assembly continued to sit and among other things, reinstituted the *Second Book of Discipline* as the standard for the government of the kirk. This remained in force until February 1645 when the Church of Scotland adopted the results of an English compromise, the *Forme of Presbyterial Church-Government* of the Westminster Assembly of Divines, as their standard.

---

[128] Burleigh, 1960:220

CHAPTER 3

THE WESTMINSTER ASSEMBLY AND THE PRESBYTERIAN OFFICES

During the mid-seventeenth century church struggles in Scotland and England, the reformed churches encountered not only royal prerogative with its preference for episcopalianism, but also independentism and parliamentary Erastianism. The controversies centred largely on the issue of authority in the church. In reaction, an all inclusive and comprehensive presbyterianism was scholastically defined by a form of church government, a confession of faith, a larger and smaller catechism, and a directory for public worship.

3.1   The calling of the Westminster Assembly of Divines

The context of the reformation of the Church of England was set by the divorce of Henry VIII. This resulted in the Church of England being separated from the papacy but subjected to the crown. The immediate background of the calling of the Westminster Assembly of Divines was the intransigence of Charles I. The long struggle which for years had marked the relationship between the English Parliament and its king, came to a head on 3 November 1641 in the "Long Parliament." There were demands from all quarters for reform. Committees were appointed to deal with specific grievances. One of these was to address religious grievances,[1] which were taken into immediate consideration. By December 1641, not merely grievances, but also religious reforms were being discussed.[2]

---

[1]   Hethrington, 1890:71
[2]   De Witt, 1969:11

A parliamentary act of 10 September 1642 ordained that the prelate form of church government would be abolished from 5 November 1643 onwards. Parliament passed an ordinance calling an Assembly of Divines to meet on 1st July 1643,[3] despite the refusal of the king to allow such an assembly. Parliament intended the primary function of this Westminster Assembly to be the reformation of church government. The ordinance calling the Assembly stated

> that such government shall be settled in the Church as may be most agreeable to God's holy word, and most apt to procure and preserve the peace of the church at home, and nearer agreement with the Church of Scotland, and other Reformed Churches abroad.[4]

A substitute for episcopacy, which was to be abolished, had to be found while the ideal of a national church was retained.[5] The first concrete steps taken by Parliament towards convening a synod was the "Grand Remonstrance," drawn up in the House of Commons on 8 November 1641 and passed with a small majority of eleven votes on 22 November.[6] Parliament stated its intentions clearly in a number of propositions. The first one stated that the intention was to reduce "that exorbitant power which the Prelates had assumed unto themselves." It also stated that it was not their purpose

> to let loose the golden reigns of Discipline and Government in the Church, to leave private persons or particular congregations to take up what form of Divine Service they please.

---

[3] It must be kept in mind that the Westminster Assembly was not a church synod as such, but an extraordinary advisory committee on religious issues called by the English Parliament (Baillie, ii.186; Rogers, 1966: 120; De Witt, 1969:18). The divines were reminded of this fact after their objection to Parliament's ordinance on excommunication in 1646 (De Witt, 1969:205).

[4] Mitchell, 1833:ix. The Assembly was charged with doctrinal reform by the ordinance only 'for the better effecting hereof, and for the vindicating and a clearing of the doctrine of the Church of England from all false calumnies and aspersions'. The general opinion was that the doctrine of the Church was Reformed and needed only to be protected from misinterpretation, whereas the government and liturgy of the Church needed readjustment (Rogers, 1966:119-120).

[5] Hethrington, 1890:102

[6] Rogers, 1966:118

They felt that there should be conformity throughout the whole realm to that order which the "Laws enjoined according to the Word of God" .... And, "the better to effect the intended Reformation," they desired a general synod

> of the most grave, pious, learned and judicious Divines of the Island, assisted by some from foreign parts professing the same religion with us, who may consider of all things necessary for the peace and good government of the Church, and represent the results of their consultations to Parliament, to be there allowed and confirmed, and receive the stamp of authority, thereby find passage and obedience throughout the kingdom.[7]

The need for Scottish assistance in the Civil War between the king and the English Parliament resulted in a Solemn League and Covenant between the Scots and Parliament. The English were obliged to yield to Scottish wishes and to make the proposed treaty a Solemn League and Covenant

> for the preservation of the Reformed religion in the Church of Scotland, in doctrine, worship, discipline, and government against our common enemies; the reformation of religion in the kingdoms of England and Ireland according to the Word of God, and example of the best reformed Churches, and for bringing the churches of God in the three kingdoms to the nearest conjunction and uniformity of religion, confession of faith, form of church government, directory for worship and catechising,[8]

and

> for the defense and preservation of the rights and privileges of the Parliament, the liberties of the kingdoms, and of the king Majesty's person and authority in the preservation and defense of the true religion and liberties of the kingdom.[9]

This ensured Scottish influence in the Westminster Assembly. On 12 October 1643, the Assembly in session revising the 16th article of the

---

[7] Rogers, 1966:118; Hethrington, 1890:88
[8] Mitchell, 1833:160; Paul, 1985:96-97
[9] Mitchell, 1833:160; Paul, 1985:96-97

Thirty Nine Articles of the Church of England, received an order from both Houses of Parliament to proceed with the matter of church government. The Assembly was instructed to

> confer and treat among themselves of such discipline and government as may be most agreeable to God's holy word, and most apt to procure and preserve the peace of the Church at home, and nearer agreement with the Church of Scotland and other Reformed Churches abroad [10]

and also to consult

> of the directory of worship, or liturgy, hereafter to be in the Church and to deliver their opinions and advices of and touching the same to both or either of the Houses of Parliament with all convenient speed.[11]

With this Assembly, the emphasis shifted from presbytery versus episcopacy and royal prerogative, to presbytery versus independency and Erastianism, and eventually, to conservative puritanism versus tolerationism. The first half of the seventeenth century was characterised by an emphasis on uniformity in doctrine and practice. This was demanded for a variety of reasons. At the Hampton Court conference of 1604, the Puritans stated "that uniformity of doctrine should be prescribed in order that Papist opinion be condemned."[12] Statesmen felt that the state could never be safe where two religions were tolerated. Sir John Eliot, in King Charles' first parliament, declared: "Religion is the bond of human society ... for where there is division in religion, as it is wrong divinity, so it makes distraction among men."[13] William Forbes, Bishop of Edinburgh, preaching before Charles on his visit to Scotland in 1633, declared: "Three things are needed to restore order - one liturgy, one catechism, one confession of faith."[14] The July 1641 Assembly of the Church of Scotland had more or less the same desire for "one confession of faith, one directory of public worship, one catechism, one form of church government in the churches of England and Scotland."[15] Leith was of the opinion that the Solemn League and Covenant "reflects

---

[10] Mitchell, 1833:160; Paul, 1985:96-97
[11] Mitchell, 1833:181
[12] MacInnes, 1966:61
[13] MacInnes, 1966:61-62
[14] MacInnes, 1966:62
[15] Ainslee, 1944:84

the conviction that the unity in a society inheres in its religion and church."[16] Uniformity was felt to be the only sure foundation for lasting peace. The issue at stake was what form such uniformity, if possible, should take. The difficulty was that the medieval conviction of the essential unity between church and state which required politicians and theologians to take note of each other, was in the process of becoming separated.[17] The battle which raged all over Europe between royal absolutism and the popular rights of the common people reached its peak in the English Civil War.

3.2 In search of a jure divino polity

3.2.1 The parties

Most of those tending toward presbyterianism and those who were "for a Congregational way"[18] in the Assembly were committed to the *jure divino* principle in establishing the polity of the church. The Erastians in the Assembly denied that *jus divinum* could be applied to any form of church government, yet they, in turn, presented their own kind of divine right of the state. They were also bound by Parliament's own requirement, laid down in the fifth rule, on the conduct of the members of the Assembly that stated: "What any man undertakes to prove as necessary, he shall make good out of Scripture."[19] Deep ecclesiological differences, however, could not be obscured by the initial agreement to the Scripture principle.[20]

What is often referred to as the *Presbyterian party* in the Assembly represented no homogenous group. There may have been a common commitment to the Scripture principle and to a national church, but it was not clear, at least at the beginning of the debates on church government, that the majority of Puritans were presbyterians. The "Puritans" represented that movement within the Church of England that was characterised by a desire for further reformation of the church and her discipline, a commitment to Scripture as the necessary basis of that

---

[16] Leith, 1978:5
[17] Paul, 1985:15, 23
[18] Paul, 1985:102
[19] Lightfoot, xiii.4
[20] De Witt, 1969:61

reformation, and an unwillingness to separate from the national church.[21] Paul maintained that in the early stages of the debates there was still a great deal of fluidity in the parties. It appears that a great majority may have preferred a moderate episcopy.[22] During the rule of Mary I, two groups distinguished themselves amongst the English refugees who settled in the Rhinelands. Theologically both groups professed an allegiance to Calvin. Division came because of their primary allegiance. The Anglican group under the leadership of Dr Cox was committed to the form of the official church as established by the English government. The group under the leadership of John Knox insisted that God, through His Scripture, had indicated the manner of church worship and organisation, and that God's will, as they understood it, was primary.[23] Only about six of the so-called English presbyterians were more or less whole-hearted in their support of the Scots' Discipline. These were Charles Herle, Richard Vines, Edward Reynolds, Thomas Temple, Lazarus Seaman, and Herbert Palmer - and of these, Baillie complained that Herle sympathised with independency.[24] They held in common a fear of anarchy because of the increase in sects, the "gathering of churches" and their threat of social destruction.[25] They had not as yet realised the possibility of a toleration of sects.[26] This fear of the sects and its consequences was probably one of the major contributing factors that caused the English presbyterians to move closer to the Scottish form of church government rather than the conviction of a *jure divino* polity. What was propagated by the successful charismatic New Model Army under leadership of Cromwell suggested changes in "Church and State that went far beyond the original causes of the struggle."[27] Although not members of the Assembly, the Scots Commis-

---

[21] Rogers, 1966:59 footnote 1; cf. Paul, 1985:101
[22] Paul, 1985:30; cf. also Paul, 1985:29 footnote 51; Kirby, 1964:418, 419; Ainslee, 1944:7
[23] Rogers, 1966:64
[24] Kirby, 1964:419; Baillie, ii.62, 67
[25] Paul, 1985:115
[26] Kirby, 1964:426
[27] Paul, 1985:121. Reaction to the settled order during the last two decades of the sixteenth century is found in the works of Thomas Cartwright and Robert Brown. Cartwright was called the father of English Presbyterianism and Brown the father of Inde-

sioners - especially the ministers Alexander Henderson, Samuel Rutherford, George Gillespie, Robert Baillie, and the lawyer Johnston of Warriston - attended and took part in the deliberations. Their polity was stated in the Solemn League and Covenant - complete religious uniformity throughout the nations of the British Isles on the basis of their own presbyterian system of church government - as the *jure divino* example.[28] The "seat of church power" for strict presbyterians was found in the officers in their hierarchy of congregation or parish, presbytery, classis and synods.[29]

The *Independents*, more or less in agreement with the presbyterians as to the officers in the church, held the entire power of government to belong to each separate congregation. Their view was that church discipline was the responsibility of the whole congregation.[30] They held a more or less middle way between the sects and presbyterianism. Goodwin, an independent, reacted to any notion of brownism which Assembly members may have thought to exist amongst the Independents, and he proposed "a middle way betwixt that called brownisme and that that [sic] it may be hath too much countenance."[31] The way "that it may be hath too much countenance" could have referred to either "presbytery" or a "clerical authority."[32] Presbyterianism presented no less of a threat to their system of church government than episcopacy had done before. Paul pointed out that "within the context of the political situation they moved from a position that had been at least sympathetic to uniformity to an enthusiastic support of religious tolerance."[33] The leading Independents were Thomas Goodwin, Philip Nye, Jeremiah Burroughs, William Bridge, and Sidrach Simpson.

---

pendentism (Beveridge, 1904:9). The Separatists or Brownists, the extreme side of the Independents, denied the possibility of reform from within the church (Rogers, 1966:67).
[28] Paul, 1985:116
[29] Kirby, 1964:420
[30] Paul, 1985:103
[31] As quoted by De Witt, 1969:70
[32] De Witt, 1969:76; Paul, 1985:153
[33] Paul, 1985:122

Those with *Erastian* sympathies in the Assembly did not favour a specific ecclesiastical polity. They were convinced that the church must be subject to the state. The Erastians in the Assembly and Parliament denied the ministers the authority proper to their spiritual offices in the church.[34] They contended that punishment of offences, whether of a civil or of religious nature, belonged to the magistrate.[35] Thomas Coleman, John Lightfoot, and the lawyer, John Selden, were the main representatives of this viewpoint in the Assembly and espoused an attitude representative of Parliament's own view that final authority in ecclesiastical matters rested with the civil authorities.[36] Though a small group in the Assembly, they enjoyed support from a large part of Parliament where power counted. On 25 April 1645, in a letter to his nephew William Spang in Holland, Baillie complained: "The most of the House of Commons are downright Erastians: they are lyke to create us much more woe than all the sectaries of England."[37]

The Assembly's discussions on church officers during the last few months of 1643 proved that the establishment of a *jure divino* polity was not something self-evident. The major difference between the parties in the Assembly centred on the issue of the seat of church authority or the "power of the keys." The question of the seat of church authority became the stumbling block on which the ideal of unanimously accepted *jure divino* polity faltered, and which eventually led to a breach between the parties during the discussions on ordination, presbytery and excommunication in the course of 1644 and 1645.

3.2.2 The debates on church officers

On 17 October, after a day of fasting, the Assembly voted to begin with the question of church government.[38] More difficult to agree upon was the method of procedure. The question was asked "whether there were a rule for government to be had in the Scripture."[39] The Erastians[40] and

---

[34] Paul, 1985:131
[35] Hethrington, 1890:134
[36] Rogers, 1966:122
[37] Baillie, ii.265
[38] Lightfoot, xiii.20
[39] Lightfoot, xiii.20
[40] Paul, 1985:137

the Independents[41] were eager to debate whether Scripture contained a rule of church government. Lightfoot, an Erastian, proposed that they should first define "a church." This was waived by the Assembly "as being too sudden a trial of the differences in opinion that are like to shew among us."[42] The viewpoint of the majority was that they should rather begin with particulars, e.g. "church officers."[43] Two years later this inductive approach was defended by the Assembly against the objection of the Independents in their 'Remonstrance'

> as to have been a part of wisdom," for they knew, "that if upon search of particulars, we could find them in Scripture, the Resolution of this question Whether there be any such Platform there, would be an easie result from the whole; but would at first entrance be found exceeding intricate and difficult.[44]

The 'Remonstrance' referred to is *A Copy of a Remonstrance Lately Delivered into the Assembly. Declaring the Grounds and Reasons of their declining to bring into the Assembly their Modell of Church-Government (London, 1645).*

3.2.2.1 The pastor

The following church officers were distinguished by the three committees: apostles, prophets, evangelists, pastors[45] and teachers, bishops or overseers, elders or presbyters, deacons and widows.[46] The final decision as laid down in *The Forme of Presbyterian Church-Government* distinguished the extra-ordinary offices - the apostles, evangelists and prophets - from the "ordinary and perpetual" offices, viz. the pastor, teacher, other church-governors, and deacons.[47] The divines

---

[41] Lightfoot, xiii.20; Beveridge, 1904:56
[42] Lightfoot, xiii.20
[43] Lightfoot, xiii.20
[44] As quoted by De Witt, 1969:65
[45] It appears that the Westminster Assembly preferred the concept of pastor to that of minister. The word pastor was used in the *Forme of Presbyterial-Church Government*, except when reference was made to "ministers of the gospel" and in the part that dealt with ordination.
[46] Lightfoot, xiii:23, 30
[47] Mair, 1913:172

agreed that the office of the pastor was a continuing and necessary office in the church.[48] It was accepted that the office of pastor was to feed, which included preaching and teaching, to convince, to reprove, to exhort, and to comfort, as well as to catechise.[49] It was agreed that it belonged to the pastor to pray when he preached, something which the bishops did not allow.[50] It was also agreed that a part of the office of the pastor was to care for the poor.[51] In addition, the task of the minister, as eventually circumscribed in *The Form of Presbyterial Church-Government*, included reference to visitation of the sick, dispensing other divine mysteries, administration of the sacraments, blessing of the people from God, and "ruling over the flock as pastor."[52]

The debate on the office of the pastor was interrupted by debates on whether or not reading belonged to the pastor's office and the difference between pastor and doctor.[53] In the debates on reading, arguments appear to have been based on an ecclesiastical office from the old order in which the tradition of the threefold order of the English Church, bishop, priest, and deacon was found.[54] It is of interest to note that the participants in this debate were mainly those associated with the so-called English presbyterian group within the Assembly. Seaman, for example, observed that "this office properly belong to the deacon."[55] But, having cleared their minds as to the matter of public reading and the duty of the pastor, the divines agreed on 6 November 1643 "that the public reading of the Scripture belongs to the pastor's office."[56]

The debates on pastors and doctors lasted a week. The Independents were for "the divine institution of a Doctor in everie congregation as well as Pastor."[57] It was mainly the English who resisted the recognition of the divine institution of the doctor apart from the pastor.[58] The Scots

---

[48] Lightfoot, xiii.36
[49] Hethrington, 1890:157
[50] Lightfoot, xiii.45; Hethrington, 1890:158
[51] Lightfoot, xiii.47
[52] Mair, 1913:173
[53] Lightfoot, xiii.36, 43, 44
[54] Paul, 1985:141.
[55] Lightfoot, xiii:36
[56] Lightfoot, xiii.40; Gillespie, *Notes*, 3
[57] Baillie, ii.110
[58] Mitchell, 1833:185

steered a more or less middle way,[59] same in substance but distinct in service. No real progress had been made in the debate by the end of the day of 15 November. Dr Burgess, therefore, asked one of the Scots Commissioners to "speak in this business."[60] Alexander Henderson addressed the Assembly. Baillie indicated that the debate was conducted in terms of a *jus divinum*.[61] But Henderson cautioned moderation and advised the English divines not to be caught up in minute distinctions. Accommodation became a characteristic of the Assembly's decisions. By 17th November, as the debate continued fruitlessly, Henderson and Palmer suggested that a committee be selected to "draw up some conclusions upon which all may agree."[62] The first attempt at an accommodation, or a "temper"[63] as Lightfoot called it, presented on the 20th, was not successful. It was eventually agreed that both offices are held forth by Scripture, that there are different gifts but that they may be exercised in one person, that where there is more than one minister in a congregation, they may be assigned to several employments, and that the teacher or doctor is of most excellent use in schools and universities.[64]

Of a more complex nature was the issue of ordination.

3.2.2.2 Ordination

Disagreement in the debates on ordination touched upon the necessity of ordination, the power to ordain, the seat of ordination, and ordination to a specific charge. The Independents and the Scots demanded that ordination be for a particular charge, but they disagreed as to who should ordain - the presbytery or the particular congregation.[65] The English presbyterians agreed with the Scots that ordination should be by the

---

[59] Paul, 1985:164
[60] Lightfoot, xiii.53
[61] De Witt, 1969:74
[62] De Witt, 1969:76
[63] Lightfoot, xiii.58
[64] Mair, 1913:173-174
[65] Kirby, 1964:423

presbytery, but that it should be *sine titulo*,[66] as their own ordination in the Anglican Church had been.[67]

To the majority of the Puritans in the Assembly, ordination was of great importance. To the Independents, ordination did not pose a problem. William Bridge urged that properly qualified candidates should be allowed to preach for the present without ordination. To Thomas Goodwin, ordination was not of such consequence that it must precede a call, and he asked whether it was "absolutely necessary to the essential of a mans [sic] being a minister."[68] The opposition view was aptly expressed by Obadiah Sedgewick on 11th January 1644, "that a minister cannot be a minister without it."[69] In addition, imposition of hands in ordination was held to be absolutely essential.[70]

The Assembly spent most of January debating the power of ordination and the seat of ordination, the main protagonists being the English presbyterians and the Independents. The issue at stake was the question of whether the power of ordination was in the apostles by virtue of their office or by virtue of the gospel entrusted to them.[71] To the Independents, the power of ordination was found in the election by the congregation. The conservative Puritans in the Assembly, in turn, could not accept any rule on ordination that might indicate a challenge to the validity of their ordination as it had been traditionally administered in England.[72] By the end of January the Assembly could still not reach a

---

[66] I.e. without title, without a specific ecclesiastical charge or incumbency (Paul, 1985:317).
[67] Kirby, 1964:423
[68] Paul, 1985:144
[69] Lightfoot, xiii.109
[70] Paul, 1985:144
[71] Paul, 1985:202. A proposition brought in by the second committee and debated on 2nd January read: "1. Apostles themselves had power to ordain officers in all churches, and to appoint evangelists to ordain, Act.vi.3, and xiv.23, Tit.i.5. 2. They had power to order all the service and worship of God, as might make most for edification, 1 Cor.xi. *per totum*, especially 23.28.34, 1 Timii.8.12, 2 Cor.xi.28, 1 Cor.xiv.26.37.40, 1 Cor.xvi.1,2. 3. To determine controversies of faith and cases of conscience in all churches, either 'viva voce,' or by writing, Act.xv. per totum, and xvi.4, and xxi.25, 1 Cor.vii per totum, Gal.v.2,3" (Lightfoot, xiii.70; 98-99).
[72] Paul, 1985:315

conclusion on the seat of ordination that was to the satisfaction of all parties. The matter was laid aside for the time being.

On 18th March 1644 the Assembly returned to the problem of ordination. After Dr Temple reported the third committee's findings on ordination,[73] an altogether new difficulty presented itself.[74] It was the second proposition that brought forth an unexpectedly bitter debate. The proposition stated: "That no one be ordained to that office (as minister) without a designation to such particular congregation or charge, Acts xiv.23, Tit. i.3, Acts xx.17.28."[75] Once again the fear that doubt could be cast on the validity of their ordination arose from this radical challenge to the orders into which most English clergymen had been ordained.[76] In their resistance to the proposition they countered both the Independents and the Scots, to whom election to a charge was an integral part of being ordained as a minister.

The debate on ordination finished on 22nd March after what Lightfoot called "a great deal of time and tug."[77] By 3 April, Dr Burgess presented the twelve propositions which the Assembly was ready to submit to Parliament as the doctrinal basis for ordination in the Church of England. On 19 April a draft of the Directory was submitted to the Assembly. The whole was presented to Parliament as the "first-fruits of the Assembly."

The final version of the "Doctrine of Ordination" attempted to satisfy the various parties. In accordance with reformed conviction it was emphasised that no "man ought to take upon himself the office of a minister of the word without a lawful calling and that ordination itself is always to be continued in the church."[78] Following the *Second Book of Discipline* and the conviction of the majority in the Assembly, ordination had to be by imposition of hands, and with fasting by "those presbyters to whom it doth belong."[79] With some restraint another important reformed principle was stated: "It is agreeable to the word, and very expedient,

---

[73] Lightfoot, xiii.218
[74] Paul, 1985:317
[75] Lightfoot, xiii.218
[76] Paul, 1985:317
[77] Beveridge, 1904:64
[78] Mair, 1913:180
[79] Mair, 1913:180

that such as are to be ordained ministers, be designed to some particular church, or other ministerial charge." The candidate was to be examined and approved by those by whom he was to be ordained. He could not be ordained in a congregation if that congregation "can show just cause of exception against him."[80] Careful formulation was needed. The Independents and the Scots were on the same side recognising that the congregation had a right in approving the person to be its minister. The opposition appears to have been prepared to invest that authority in presbyteries, and to have expected them to act with similar power as the earlier bishops. Finally, under the heading "Touching the Power of Ordination", it was stated that ordination was an act of the presbytery, and that it did not belong to one congregation "to assume itself all and sole power in ordination." At this stage, when the work on ordination was completed, the Assembly had not as yet declared what kind of presbytery there would be. The conclusion eventually reached was that

> Because there is in Scripture example of an ordination in a presbytery over divers congregations; as in the church of Jerusalem, where were many congregations: these many congregations were under one presbytery, and this presbytery did ordain.[81]

In the debates on ordination it seems that there was a concern for reaffirming ministerial authority. The chapters dealing with ordination in the *Form of Presbyterial Church-Government* confirms the distinction of the minister as a clerical class separate from the rest of the church.

3.2.2 3 The elder

In the Westminster Assembly the divine institution of the office of the ruling elder was challenged. Ruling elders were an essential part of the Scottish church discipline and were also found in the Independent churches, but they were not found in the English church.[82] The debate on the ruling elder started on 22nd November and was based on a proposition brought forward by the second committee which stated "that besides those presbyters that rule well, and labour in the word and doctrine, there be other presbyters who especially apply themselves to

---

[80] Mair, 1913:180
[81] Mair, 1913:181
[82] Kirby, 1964:424

ruling though they labour not in word and doctrine."[83] The debates centred on the texts provided to prove the proposition. The first text was 1 Tim 5:17: "Let the elders that rule well be counted worthy of double honour, especially they who labour in word and doctrine." Some interpreted the verse to refer to the civil magistrate.[84] Others felt it referred only to preaching elders. To some the verse suggested preaching elders and presiding preaching bishops.[85] When, on 24 November, Dr Burgess proposed that a way must be found "in a prudential course" which would satisfy those who could not establish "a *Jus divinum* upon that which hath not an Infallible, Impregnable foundation," Nye objected to establishing the office on such grounds.[86] Neither Rom. 12, nor 1 Cor. 12:28 could convince the "dissenters." In order to find a solution to the debate, Lightfoot proposed that they first attend to the work of the ruling elder, but in line with his Erastian convictions, he warned that if their debate should indicate "that ecclesiastical censure" was in the elders' power, it would be denied.[87] Henderson recommended at the end of the day, on 7 December, that a committee be chosen to draw up "how far we might agree, and then to draw up the elders' office."[88] This committee sat in the afternoon for that purpose. The next morning it was reported:

> 1. Christ hath instituted a government, and governors, ecclesiastical in the church. 2. Christ hath furnished some in his church with gifts for government, and with commission to exercise the same, when called thereunto. 3. It is agreeable and warranted by the word of God, that some others beside the ministers should join with the ministers in the government of the church. Rom xii.7,8, 1 Cor xii.28.[89]

Some agreed with the proposals but not with the proof texts. Eventually the propositions and the texts were approved and a last attempt by

---

[83] Lightfoot, xiii.60
[84] Lightfoot, xiii.60
[85] For example "old Mr. Wilkinson" and Henry Hall (Paul, 1985:169, 170).
[86] De Witt, 1969:79
[87] Lightfoot, xiii.74
[88] Lightfoot, xiii.75
[89] Lightfoot, xiii.76

Whittacre and Gillespie to have 1 Tim 5:17 added as proof text failed.[90] As proposed by Dr Burgess, it was decided not to discuss the texts until after the work of the elder was debated. The debate on the work of the ruling elder continued until 14th December when "the subject was laid aside for the present."[91] The subject of the ruling elder surfaced again on 3 May 1644. It was first proposed that there should be at least one ruling elder in every congregation. This was opposed by the Scottish Commissioners as in reality not forming a congregational eldership.[92]

In the completed *Form of Presbyterial Church-Government*, the word "elder" was used strictly in the sense of the minister or pastor. The officers whom reformed churches "commonly call Elders" are referred to in this document as "other church-governors."[93] The Assembly found that Christ, who instituted government and governors ecclesiastical in the church, furnished some in his church "with gifts for government, and with commission to execute the same when called thereunto, who are to join the minister in the government of the church."[94] Scripture references to support the final findings of the Assembly ignored the traditional appeal to 1 Tim 5:17, but added 2 Chron 19:8,9, and 10 as a reference for elders appointed in the "Jewish church" to assist the priests and Levites in the government of the church.[95]

3.2.2.4 The deacon

The proposition, "that it was the office of the deacon to take special care to distribute to the necessaties of the poor,"[96] was read on 14th December and the debate started the next day. Several of the divines were of the opinion that the office of the deacon was not of divine institution, but that it was of a temporary nature. Others held a view that was closer to the office of the deacon in the old order of bishop, priest and deacon. For example, Mr. Wilkinson sr. held that the deacon was an officer subordinate to the pastor as the Levites were to the priests and "subservient to the pastor as far as his ability and authority will extend." He held that the deacon be continued in the church "1. Because the poor

---

[90] Lightfoot, xiii.77
[91] Lightfoot, xiii.83
[92] Hethrington, 1890:206
[93] Mair, 1913:174
[94] Mair, 1913:174
[95] Mair, 1913:174
[96] Lightfoot, xiii.83

shall always [be with us]. 2. Because God hath promised a blessing upon the contribution to the poor."[97] In addition, the deacon had to pray, read the word, baptise and visit the sick. In Dr Smith's opinion the deacon had a "greater work." With regard to ordination, deacons were to be approved, set apart, chosen and examined. They had the "imposition of hands" and after ordination they were allowed to baptise and preach.[98] The proposal, "Whether the deacon be [allowed] to assist the pastor in preaching and administering the sacraments," was voted negatively.[99] By 28 December the proof texts, 1 Tim 3:8,9; Rom12:8 and Acts 6 to support the proposition that the office of the deacon was to be continued in the church, were accepted. The remaining issue was the office of the widows which was not accepted as a separate office.

In the *Form of Presbyterial Church-Government* the deacon is dealt with very briefly as being Scriptural and permanent.[100] It further stipulates that it did not belong to this office to preach the word or to administer the sacraments. Its function was to take special care in distributing the necessities to the poor.[101]

The offices of elder and deacon were not discussed in terms of a ministry in the church. The matter of parity between minister, elder and deacon, therefore, also did not receive any consideration. The "other church governors" and deacons were rather considered as officials who were assigned certain tasks in order to assist the ministry of the pastor - much in line with the Anglican deacon's relationship to the bishop.

3.2.3   The seat of church power

Inherent in the differences between the parties and a major stumbling block to unanimously achieving a jure divino church polity, was the issue of the seat of church power. The presbyterian position had to be maintained against the Independents on the one side and against the Erastians on the other.

---

[97] Lightfoot, xiii.90
[98] Lightfoot, xiii:90
[99] Lightfoot, xiii:91
[100] Mair, 1913:174
[101] Mair, 1913:174

Goodwin's argument in the discussion on the "power of the keys" as early as 20 October 1643, was that "the opinions of some is that all power being in Jesus Christ he hath given it to officers and from them to the church ... Other men goe another way."[102] The majority in the Assembly maintained that the keys were not given to the church but to the apostles. The speech of Simpson, also an Independent, on the issue went to the heart
of the matter. According to him, Matt 16:19 was spoken to Peter as a believer.[103] The major difference between the viewpoints was that the Presbyterians taught that authority in the church resided in the office-bearers in their assemblies; the Independents taught that it is seated rather in the congregation itself, or in the congregation together with the office-bearers.[104] Paul found behind this debate on the keys

> a very strong and traditional concern for maintaining the distinction between clerical and lay persons and for reaffirming ministerial authority, against the Independents' insistence that ecclesiastical power should be corporatively in the hands of the whole congregation.[105]

This essential difference between the Presbyterians and the Independents came to a head in the debate on the presbytery, which started on 5 February 1644 and lasted for almost a year. The subject matter concerned the establishment of the presbytery and the subordination of the church courts.

The first issue centred on the crucial proposition "that there may be many congregations under one presbytery, as in the church at Jerusalem." On 19 January 1644 Dr Burgess reported for the first committee concerning the presbytery. The propositions were: "1. The Scripture holdeth out a presbytery in a church. 1 Tim iv.14, Acts xv. 2.4.6. 2. A presbytery consisteth of ministers of the word, and such other public officers, as have already voted to have a share in the government of the church."[106] On the 22nd a third proposition was added: "That there may be many congregations under one presbytery, as in the

---

[102] As quoted by De Witt, 1969:68
[103] Lightfoot, xiii.32ff.
[104] De Witt, 1969:67
[105] Paul, 1985:147
[106] Lightfoot, xiii.115

church at Jerusalem."[107] This last proposition was "most vehemently" opposed by the Independents.[108] The Assembly voted that the example of the church at Jerusalem was the first proof for the proposition.[109] The second proof voted on 25th April was the example of the church of Ephesus.[110] It was argued that these churches consisted of more than one congregation, and all these congregations were under one presbyterial government.[111]

After some delay the Assembly returned to the issue of church government on 4 September 1644 to debate the proposition that "it is lawful and agreeable to the word of God, that the church must be governed by several sorts of Assemblies."[112] This was passed on 6 September. This proposition was not merely a statement on a specific preference in church polity; it acquired the status of an article of faith. It was taken up not only in the *Form of Presbyterial Church-Government*,[113] but also in the *Westminster Confession of Faith*.[114]

On 13 September, 1644 the divines commenced debating the different ecclesiastical assemblies "in this method, synodical, classical, and congregational."[115] More troublesome was the question of a subordination of assemblies, taken up by the Assembly on 23 September 1644. On 1st October the Assembly voted that "it is lawful and agreeable to the word of God, that there be a subordination of congregational, classical, provincial, and national assemblies for the government of the church."[116] The proposition went against the Independents' conviction of the "power of particular congregations."[117] On 2nd October it was voted as a proof for the proposition "that Matt xviii, holding forth the

---

[107] Lightfoot, xiii.116
[108] Lightfoot, xiii.131
[109] Gillespie, *Notes*, 38
[110] Lightfoot, xiii.254
[111] Mair, 1913:178-179
[112] Lightfoot, xiii.309; Gillespie, *Notes*, 65
[113] Mair, 1913:176
[114] Westminster Confession of Faith, XXXI.I
[115] Gillespie, *Notes*, 70
[116] Gillespie, *Notes*, 84
[117] De Witt, 1969:130

subordination of an offending brother to a particular church, it doth also, by a parity of reason, prove a subordination of a congregation to superior assemblies."[118]

Thus the Westminster Divines defined the church, on the basis of a literal biblical appeal, as an all inclusive and comprehensive institution, ecclesiologically considered in terms of the universal church. With the seat of church power established, attention needed to be given to the nature of church authority.

It was on the subject of excommunication that the Assembly experienced its greatest challenge to the autonomy of the church. The main cause of the difficulties was the interference with the freedom of the church to exclude unworthy persons from the Lord's Supper. Debates on excommunication started on 14 October 1644 and on the 25th it was proposed "that the ruling officers of a particular congregation have power authoritatively to suspend from the Lord's table a person not yet cast out of the church."[119] Two papers containing the advice of the Assembly on excommunication and a directory for admonition, excommunication, and absolution[120] were presented to the two Houses of Parliament on 4 February 1645.[121] The House of Commons, however, required of the Assembly specific lists of what sins or disabilities should disqualify a person from the sacrament.[122] On 17th April the Commons accepted a resolution placing in the hands of the elderships the power to examine and judge such persons as should be kept from the sacrament upon the basis of the sins enumerated.[123] But Parliament still had to settle the way in which such jurisdiction was to be executed. On 13 May 1645 the Commons adopted a resolution which aroused opposition:

> If any Person, suspended from the Lord's Supper, shall find himself grieved with the Proceeding before the Eldership of any Congregation, he shall have Liberty to appeal to the Classical

---

[118] Gillespie, *Notes*, 86
[119] Gillespie, *Notes*, 96
[120] A copy is printed in Hall and Hall, *Paradigms in Polity. Classic Readings in Reformed and Presbyterian Government*, 1994:260ff.
[121] De Witt, 1969:180
[122] Paul, 1985:496
[123] De Witt, 1969:181

Assembly; from thence to the Provincial; from thence to the National; and from thence to the Parliament.[124]

This offensive paragraph was included in the first parliamentary ordinance for scandal which appeared on 20 October 1645 under the title: *An Ordinance of the Lords and Commons Assembled in Parliament Together withthe Rules and Directions concerning Suspension from the Sacrament of the Lord's Supper In Cases of Ignorance and Scandal.*[125] What was a greater offense to the Divines was the manner in which Parliament dealt with unenumerated sins. In March 1646 a new ordinance of Parliament dealing with various aspects of church government was printed. It was *An Ordinance of the Lords and Commons Assembled in Parliament For Keeping Scandalous persons from the Sacrament of the Lord's Supper, the enabling of Congregations for the choice of Elders, and Supplying of Defects in former Ordinances, and Directions of Parliament concerning Church-Government.*[126] It required the choosing of commissioners by Parliament for every province "to judge of scandalous offences (not enumerated in any Ordinance of Parliament) to them presented."[127] It was stated in the fourteenth article:

> In every Province persons shall be chosen by the Houses of Parliament, that shall be Commissioners to judge of scandalous offences (not enumerated in any Ordinance of Parliament to them presented; And that the Eldership of that Congregation, where the said offence was committed, shall upon examination and proof of such scandalous offence (in like manner as is done in the case of offences enumerated) certify the same to the Commissioners, together with the proof taken before them, and before the said certificate, the party accused shall have liberty to make such defence as he shall think fit before the said Eldership, and also before the Commissioners, before any certificate, shall be made to the Parliament. And if the said Commissioners after examination of all parties, shall determine

---

124 As quoted by De Witt, 1969:181
125 De Witt, 1969:188
126 De Witt, 1969:192
127 De Witt, 1969:192

the offence so presented and proved to be scandalous, and the same shall certify to the Congregation, the Eldership thereof may suspend such person from the Sacrament of the Lord's Supper, in like manner as in cases enumerated in any Ordinance of Parliament.[128]

This stipulation was fortunately eliminated in a new ordinance of 9 June 1646.[129] Besides strong reactions by way of petitions, the Assembly's view on this issue was expressed in the *Confession of Faith*. The introductory paragraph to Article XXX *Of Church Censure* read "The Lord Jesus, as king and head of his church, hath therein appointed a government in the hand of church-officers, distinct from the civil magistrate."[130] The right of the church to excommunication was asserted in this article. In Article XXX1 *Of Synods and Councils* the right of government by synods and control over ecclesiastical matters was asserted. These two articles, however, were omitted from the "Articles of the Christian Religion," Parliament's official March 1648 publication of the Confession.[131]

3.3 The Westminster Assembly and presbyterianism

The development of a reformed ecclesiology in the Westminster Assembly was conditioned by political and ecclesiological factors and considerations. In their struggle for a presbyterian polity the Scottish Commissioners and the English Puritans had to face Independents on the one side and parliamentary Erastians on the other. The debates on church government centred on the question of the representation of Christ in the church. Three issues determined developments, viz., the need to establish a reformed form of church government for the national church, the conviction of the essential relationship between church and society which did not allow for a plurality of churches, and the threat of state control to the autonomy of the church. In response to these issues, and in line with the *Second Book of Discipline*, the Westminster Assembly adopted a system of church government in which the church

---

128 As quoted by De Witt, 1969:192
129 De Witt, 1969:226
130 Westminster Confession of Faith, XXX.I
131 De Witt, 1969:238

was conceived as a constituted institution with authority centralized in courts hierarchically ordered. The church institution representing the universal church replaced the local congregation as complete manifestation of the universal church with its ministries and life in faith as ecclesiological starting point. This position was scripturally and confessionally reasoned. The presbytery was confirmed as the basic unit in the government of the church. Ministers were considered first of all to be members of the presbytery and only secondary related to the congregation. The replacement of the rule of Christ through his Word and Spirit using office-bearers with representation of officers-in-assembly as found in Scottish Presbyterian ecclesiology was maintained.

With the Westminster Assembly documents, the adaptation of the episcopal system to the reformed conviction of the government of the church was completed. *Episcopé* related to an individual was replaced by *episcopé* exercised by presbyters in hierarchical assemblies or courts. What remained unresolved in this adaptation was the position and function of the reformed offices.

3.4 Further developments

A *Directory of Public Worship* was completed and submitted to the English Parliament in 1644. The *Form of Presbyterial Church-Government* was completed in 1645 and ratified by the English Parliament in January 1646. By 1647 a *Confession of Faith* and the *Shorter* and *Larger Catechisms* were completed. Interestingly, while the *Westminster Standards*, drawn up with a view to the Church of England, received a luke-warm reception and eventually had no future there, the Scots were committed to a hoped-for uniformity in the churches of Scotland, England and Ireland in matters of church government, confession of faith, directory of worship and catechism. As the Westminster documents were completed, they were accepted by the General Assembly of the Church of Scotland. The *Form of Presbyterial Church-Government* became the guiding standard for Scottish presbyterian churches and presbyterian churches world wide.

Things did not go well for the presbyterian programme in either country. In Scotland, Cromwell only tolerated it and the General Assembly was dissolved in 1653 by his soldiers.[132] In England, the *Form of Presbyterial Church-Government* was put into operation half-heartedly and eventually put aside.[133] After the restoration of Charles II, son of Charles I, episcopacy was again established in both England and Scotland in 1661. When James VII(II) was compelled to abdicate after the Revolution of 1688/89, William III of Orange and Mary became the sovereigns of Great Britain, and presbyterian church government was finally established in Scotland in 1690.

Seventeenth century Scotland was an age of extreme contrasts. On the one hand there was intense religious intolerance with its emphasis on uniformity in religion and accompanied political conflict, burning of witches, stagnation in trade and agriculture, high unemployment, desperate poverty,[134] and the "Killing Times" - the severe and indiscriminate persecution, after 1661, aimed at destroying the uncompromising presbyterians who had disowned the king and state as uncovenanted.[135] On the other hand, the ideals of the reformers regarding education of all the young received attention with schools in almost every burgh and universities open to all.[136] In addition, Scotland enjoyed a period of continuously stable government. Results were obtained in law and order for which credit is given to the bishops, ministers and kirk-sessions and their persistent work in alliance with the central and local authorities.[137] It was the century that saw the formation of the first presbytery in Ireland on 10 June, 1642 at Carrickfergus, north of Belfast, and the formation of the allegedly first permanent Presbyterian congregation in North America in 1677.[138] The keynote to the new age introduced by the Revolution was set by the new king's advice to the first General Assembly to meet in thirty-seven years: "Moderation is what religion enjoines, neighbouring churches expect from you, and we recommend to you."[139]

---

[132] Ainslee, 1940:26
[133] Burleigh, 1960:226
[134] Mackie, 1966:191, 194
[135] Cameron, 1993:458; Pryde, 1962:19, 20
[136] Pryde, 1962:35ff.
[137] Mackie, 1963:196
[138] Davies, 1965:70, 82
[139] Davies, 1965:74

CHAPTER 4

THE CHURCH AS AN ESTABLISHED INSTITUTION

The ecclesiological premise of the church as institution in Scottish presbyterianism is reflected in the continued struggle for the spiritual independence of the church from civil domination, and the accompanied conviction that the church as institution must be in sole control of all aspects of its government. Different conceptions developed reflecting different views on the right of the church to regulate itself. One view was based on a pragmatic assumption; the other sought a scripturally justified model. Both maintained a common sense approach in dealing with difficulties. The similarities, however, were unable to maintain the unity of the church for two reasons. On the one hand, the understanding of the relationship between church and state, patronage, and conflicting approaches to religion became the major causes of secession in the Scottish church. On the other hand, the question of establishment and the spiritual independence of the church were major stumbling blocks on the road to reunion. In this ecclesiastical development there was no time for the consideration of the reformed offices as ministries serving the direct rule of Christ.

4.1   The Moderates and the church

During the eighteenth century the question of the government of the church arose because of tension between the conviction that it was the right of the local congregation to elect its own minister and the requirements of the law of the land. This question touched upon church discipline in general and the authority of the general assembly in particular. This difficulty went hand in hand with the question of the right of the church to control its own affairs - thus with the relationship between church and state and conflicting theological viewpoints.

From the Reformation until 1874, there was a more or less perpetual struggle in the Church of Scotland against patronage as imposed by the State on the Church.[1] In 1649 patronage was abolished for the first time. Ministers of parishes were henceforth called with the consent of the congregation.[2] With the Restoration of Episcopacy in 1660 patronage was restored. All the provisions of the Act of 1649 were repealed.[3]

The first Scottish Parliament that met after the Revolution of 1688 declared prelacy to be "a great and insurpportable [sic] grievance to the nation, contrary to the inclinations of the generality of the people ever since the Reformation."[4] Parliament ratified the Westminster Confession of Faith. In 1690, according to the establishment, which had been given to it in 1592, the presbyterian form of church government was re-established.[5] In addition, Parliament appointed the first meeting of the General Assembly to be held on the third Tuesday of October 1690.[6] The Act of 1690 concerning patronage deprived patrons of the right of presentation and gave the power of nomination to the "heritors of the parish being Protestants and elders."[7] The congregations were given the right to approve or disapprove the appointment of a minister. If they disapproved, reasons had to be given to the presbytery, which was to be the final judge.

In 1712, the Parliament of the recently united Kingdom, apparently without any consultation with the Church of Scotland,[8] put the law of patronage back into the Statute Book. The Act restored the rights of lay patrons, and required and obliged presbyteries to receive any qualified person presented to a parish.[9] The Act made no reference to any call or consent on the part of the people.[10]

---

[1] Fleming, 1927:268
[2] Fleming, 1927:269
[3] Fleming, 1927:269
[4] M'Kerrow, 1841:2
[5] Donaldson, 1974:260
[6] Donaldson, 1974:260
[7] Fleming, 1927:269
[8] Steward, 1984:18
[9] Herron, 1985:51
[10] Fleming, 1927:270

Initially no great disturbances were experienced, and crown patronage was exercised with respect for popular opinion.[11] But things were to change after 1725. Leaders in the church courts began to find themselves caught in a difficult position between the law of patronage on the one side, and the right of the congregation on the other.[12] Patrons began to insist on their legal rights and to ignore the wishes of the congregation. Theological controversies seemed to have made it desirable to have representatives of one's own persuasion in the General Assembly, and patrons appeared to have made this the primary, if not the sole, criterion when presenting a minister.[13] Congregations, at the same time, became more conscious of their rights. The General Assembly, in turn, began to enforce the Patronage Act with increasing vigour, and in 1729 the Assembly went so far as to disregard the popular "call."[14] Forced settlements of ministers by what was called "Riding Committees" became the practice. When presbyteries refused to act against popular feeling in the ordination of an unpopular presentee, the General Assembly or its Commission appointed a committee of members from outside the presbytery to proceed with the induction of the unwanted minister. This was first done in 1729.[15]

The different practices of settling a minister followed by presbyteries after the right of presentation fell to them *jure devolutum*[16] called for attention. In some cases presbyteries acted as patrons themselves in the presentation of a minister, in others the right was given to the congregation to elect its minister. In order to obtain uniformity in practice, the General Assembly of 1731, under the Barrier Act,[17] sent a proposal

---

[11] Drummond and Bullock, 1973:39-40
[12] M'Kerrow, 1941:32
[13] Benton, 1969:126
[14] Benton, 1969:127
[15] M'Kerrow, 1841:33; Drummond and Bullock, 1973:40
[16] This happened when the Crown did not make a presentation within six months (Herron, 1985:52).
[17] The Barrier Act was introduced in 1697 to prevent hasty action. The requirement was that an innovation affecting the constitution and/or liturgy of the Church of Scotland had to be sent to the presbyteries and it could only be enacted when their consent had been secured (Drummond and Bullock, 1973:12).

to presbyteries that in vacant parishes the choice should be made by the elders and protestant heritors, and in royal burghs by the magistrate, town councils and elders. This was accepted by the Assembly of 1732.[18] The congregations were, according to this arrangement, not involved in the election of a minister but could approve or disapprove of the presentee,[19] much as they could under the Act of 1690.

This modest adjustment went against the convictions of those who wanted the rights of the congregation in the election of the minister to be fully restored. This arrangement of 1731 contributed to the secession of Ebenezer Erskine and his followers from the Church of Scotland. Erskine, who led the secession, was convinced that "God's promise of guidance was not given to heritors or patrons, but to the church."[20] They formed what was called "The Associate Presbytery" (later the "Associate Synod.")[21]

More than just opposition to patronage was involved. What was at stake was the development of conflicting approaches to the reformed religion. The different approaches were represented at the heresy trials of John Simson, Professor of Divinity at Glasgow University, and the "Marrow Controversy" of 1718-1723. Both were symptomatic of the changes of the age. The first represented the rise of rationalism (not that Simson's teaching actually reached the deism and rationalism of the eighteenth century), and the second represented the first signs of the rise of an evangelical party in the Church of Scotland.[22]

In 1714 charges of Socinianism and Arminianism were raised against Simson. The General Assembly of 1717 found him guilty of venting "some opinions not necessary to be taught in divinity," using doubtful expressions and adopting hypotheses tending "to attribute too much to natural reason and the power of corrupt nature."[23] He was told to be more careful in future. In 1726 he was accused of Socinianism and Arianism. He was condemned and suspended in 1729, but not deposed.

---

[18] Drummond and Bullock, 1973:31; M'Kerrow, 1841:38
[19] M'Kerrow, 1841:38
[20] Benton, 1969:128
[21] In 1747 this church split into the Burgher and Anti-Burgher Synods.
[22] Drummond and Bulloch, 1973:37
[23] Drummond and Bulloch, 1973:32; Cameron, 1993:775

He was relieved of his teaching duties but retained his salary.[24] These actions by the General Assembly to the Simson case seem to reflect hidden theological sympathy.[25]

The re-publication in Scotland of *The Marrow of Modern Divinity*, which had originally been published in England in 1645, was designed to counteract the errors which Thomas Boston and several others considered prevalent in the church. Ebenezer Erskine was one of those involved in the controversy that followed. The work was condemned by the General Assembly of 1720 as incompatible with the teachings of the Westminster Confession.[26] According to Lachman, the "Marrow Controversy" may be viewed as a conflict

> between the majority in the Church of Scotland who represented in some degree a late seventeenth century tendency towards Legalism, Neonomianism, and even Arminianism in Reformed thought (which proved a seed bed for later Moderatism) and the minority who wished to return to what they considered rightly, true Reformed Orthodoxy.[27]

Erskine and his followers, however, also seemed to have revered a presbyterianism of the Covenanting type of the previous century. A *Testimony* of December 1736 reflected their sympathies. They held against the Assembly its failure to renew the Covenants, and its failure to assert the divine right of presbytery, its toleration of "Episcopal hirelings," the uncovenanted union with England, the "Yule" holidays in the courts, the condemnation of the *Marrow of Modern Divinity*, the failure to excommunicate Professor Simson, the sanctioning of sinful activities such as assemblies and balls, and the repeal of the statutes against witchcraft.[28] It seems that it was inevitable that there would be a parting of ways even if agreement on patronage were reached.

Different issues stood in tension with each other. On the one side there was a conservative Calvinism along the line of the Westminster

---

[24] Drummond and Bulloch, 1973:37
[25] Drummond and Bulloch, 1973:33; van Harten, 1986:36
[26] Lachman, 1988:276
[27] Lachman, 1988:491
[28] Pryde, 1962:98-99

Confession of Faith and the claim for the right of the congregation or the Christian people to elect their own minister. On the other side there was the fact of the law of the land and the principle of subordination of judicatories, which required obedience to the courts, which raised the question of the relationship between the church and the state and a different theological inclination. The secular spirit of "reason" made advances in Scotland as elsewhere and represented itself in the Church of Scotland in what came to be known as the Moderate party.

This party emerged as a party within the Church of Scotland during the 1750s and took the lead. Involved in the approach of the Moderates was the relationship between church and state. In order to free the church from external and political manipulation, as well as to re-introduce discipline and the authority of the General Assembly, an expedient course was taken.[29] On the one hand, the Assembly insisted on co-operation with the law of the land in return for freedom from interference.[30] On the other hand, if the church was to be strong and master in its own house, capable of dealing with the civil authority on equal terms, the power and authority of the General Assembly had to be asserted.[31] Improvement in ministers' stipend was apparently not a minor issue.[32] The Moderates' attempt to assert the church's control over its own affairs found expression in the treatment of two related issues during this period - church discipline and lay patronage.[33]

The employment of "Riding Committees" reflected badly on the General Assembly's exercise of authority. The implication was that presbyteries need not execute Assembly decisions with regard to unpopular settlements. William Robertson, who became the leader of the Moderate Party for the greater part of the eighteenth century, and his friends considered how they could best "re-establish the authority of the church."[34] The case of Thomas Gillespie brought the question of discipline and patronage to a head. He was an advocate for the election

---

[29] Chitnis, 1976:62
[30] Chitnis, 1976:62
[31] Chitnis, 1976:62
[32] Benton, 1969:129; Chitnis, 1976:61
[33] Benton, 1969:126
[34] Benton, 1969:126

of ministers by the Christian people and opposed patronage. He considered it not a grievance but "an antichristian usurpation."[35]

In 1751, the Presbytery of Dumferline, of which Gillespie was a member, could not ordain a presentee at Inverkeithing as instructed due to an insufficient quorum. Gillespie was one of those absent. The reason given was "that it is and has been since the Reformation, the principle of the church, that no minister shall be intruded into any parish contrary to the will of the congregation."[36] When the Commission of the General Assembly decided not to censure them, Robertson and his colleagues presented their *Reasons of Dissent* (often referred to as the "Manifesto" of the Moderate Party) against the Commission's ruling. Their argument was that membership to a "society" involves the acceptance of the judgement of the majority or of those entrusted with authority. This was considered especially true in presbyterian polity where the parity of ministers was balanced by subordination of judicatories.[37] The enjoyment of priviledges entails the acceptance of law and order and this was true for the church.[38] It was argued that discipline rightly enforced is part of the church's nature.[39] The principles were:

> That as Patronage is the law of the land, the courts of a national church established and protected by law, and all the individual ministers of that church are bound, as far as it depends upon exertions arising from the duties of their place, to give it effect, and that church courts betrayed their duty to the constitution when the spirit of their decision, or negligence in enforcing obedience to their order, created unnecessary obstacles to the exercise of the rights of patronage and fostered in the minds of the people the false idea that they have a right to choose their

---

[35] Struthers, 1843:34
[36] M'Kerrow, 1841:247
[37] Benton, 1969:129
[38] According to Struthers (1843:65) the sentiment was: "submission to the law of patronage was expected from all those who would be fed from the King's table."
[39] Drummond and Bullock, 1973:65

own minister, or even a negative opinion upon the nomination of the patron.[40]

The conclusion was clear; in an established church obedience to the law of the land goes hand in hand with church discipline in general and with the authority of the General Assembly in a presbyterian system of government in particular.[41] They argued that a clear distinction must be drawn between man as an individual following the light of his conscience, and man in society relinquishing certain individual rights and submitting to lawfully constituted authority.[42] As in the case of a society, it was held that

> as long as he [the member] continues in it, professes regard for it, and reaps the emoluments of it, if he refuses to obey its laws, he manifestly sets both a disorderly and dishonest part: he lays claim to the priviledges of the society, whilst he condemns the authority of it.[43]

The Moderates argued that they were not introducing a new principle of church order, but that they were merely reviving the inherent authority of the General Assembly by insisting that its decisions be carried out by synods and presbyteries. They claimed that the disobedience of a presbytery, or of a minister within a presbytery, to the lawful command of the Assembly struck at the "very root of presbyterianism."[44] Gillespie was deposed and the approach of the Assembly was that in future order would be enforced.[45] The Moderates were not so much concerned with

---

[40] As quoted by Struthers, 1843:96. When a minister was nominated to a parish by the patron, the custom was for him to preach to the congregation; a call was then signed by the congregation and presented to the presbytery, which, after sustaining the call, inducted the minister. Under the Moderates the signing of the call, which had once been essential, ceased to be (Drummond and Bullock, 1973:222).

[41] Sher and Murdoch, 1983:212

[42] Benton, 1969:129

[43] Benton, 1969:130

[44] Benton, 1969:130

[45] Drummond and Bullock, 1973:66; On the 22nd of October 1761, the Rev. Thomas Boston, Rev. Thomas Colier, and Rev. Thomas Gillespie formed themselves into a presbytery "for the relief of Christians oppressed in their christian priviledges" (Struthers, 1843:160). The United Secession Church and the Relief Church united in 1847 to form the United Presbyterian Church.

the desirability of patronage as with the fact that it was the legal method of appointing ministers to vacant parishes.[46] In addition, Robertson believed that much could be gained from the *status quo*. The suggestion was that the legal system of ministerial appointment could make possible the appointment of a certain kind of clergyman - those, for example, of a more liberal education and of higher social status than in the past.[47]

With the Moderates in the chair, the rule of Christ was not considered. The General Assembly took care of the church in accordance with existing laws. In this approach from above there was no place for the direct rule of Christ in His church. The rights of the congregation to elect its minister and the office of the elder were neglected. The emphasis was on order. The government by the Moderates, according to John McCleod

> got into the hands of the men of Broad tendency. And their leaders, without having the name of bishop, tended to exercise the governing and managing functions that were, as a rule associated with the diocesan prelate.[48]

Further on he described them as "managers of Church business."[49]

4.2 The Evangelicals and the church

The emphasis on the church as institution in an episcopal sense continued to be characteristic of Scottish ecclesiology in the midst of the Evangelical party that developed in the Scottish Church. Despite a return to Scripture, the institutional emphasis, strengthened in the continued church-state struggle, did not allow for a theological consideration of the direct rule of Christ through His Word and Spirit using office-bearers.

Besides the covenantal approach of the Seceders and the devitalised religion of so many Moderates the eighteenth century also saw the rise of Evangelicalism.[50] Various waves of religious revival were experienced in Scotland during this century. In 1741 the Seceders invited George Whitefield to Scotland. They, however, insisted that he renounce his

---

[46] Chitnis, 1976:61
[47] Chitnis, 1976:62
[48] McCleod, 1974:199
[49] McCleod, 1974:201
[50] Mackie, 1963:259

prelatic ordination, embrace presbyterianism, sign the Covenants, and restrict his preaching to their members.[51] The pulpits of the Established Church were opened to him. Apart from his work, a major revival was experienced in the Established Church parish of Cambuslang in 1742.[52] At the end of the century there was again a wave of religious awakening which touched all ranks of society.[53] Throughout Scotland men and women began to embrace a vital biblical Christianity. By the 1800s

> the Moderate tide was receding. The Enlightment ideals of reason and harmony, which had impressed the thinkers in the mid-eighteenth century, had now spent their force. The Romantic Movement had commenced, emphasizing feeling as opposed to reason, and power and versatility as opposed to the harmony of nature.[54]

Those who were mainly characterised as being opposed to patronage in the General Assembly formed what was known after 1750 as the "Popular Party" which became known during the early years of the nineteenth century as the Evangelical Party. They were strict Calvinists emphasizing "obedience to God's laws as revealed through Scripture, or as defined in the Westminster Confession."[55] The Evangelicals became the dominant party in the General Assembly by the 1830s. Between 1834 and 1843 there was, between the Moderates and the Evangelicals in the Church of Scotland, an intense and bitter contest known as the "Ten Year Conflict" in which the Evangelicals vainly sought government legislation and support for their position on patronage and evangelisation.[56] Central to this struggle was the relationship between church and state, accompanied by religious divisions which would lead to the parting of ways between the Evangelicals and the Moderates.[57]

From 1829 the Church of Scotland was confronted with a strong insistence on disestablishment. Until about 1800 the Presbyterian secession had remained loyal to the principle of national Establishment. This was to

---

[51] Cunningham, 1882, ii.313-314
[52] Cunningham, 1882, ii.316
[53] Mackie, 1963:259
[54] Brown, 1982:45
[55] Brown, 1982:47
[56] Brown, 1987:33
[57] Ross, 1988:8

change. In 1796 the General Associate Synod (Anti-Burgher) accepted a modified formula of subscription to the Westminster Confession of Faith, which emancipated the subscriber from any belief in the power of the magistrate in spiritual matters.[58] The Associate Synod (Burghers) followed the same way in 1797. Those who disagreed with these "New Lights" formed the Original Secession Church. The "New Light" Burghers and the "New Light" Anti-Burghers, in agreement with each other on the disestablishment principle, united in 1820 to form the United Secession Church. The conviction of disestablishment received attention in a sermon by Dr Andrew Marshall of the United Secession Church in 1829, which led to a powerful Voluntary Movement throughout the country. His concern was the recent measure of Catholic Emancipation in Ireland. The Roman Catholic Relief Bill was passed in the course of this same year[59] and freed the Roman Catholics from most of their civil disabilities.[60] In order to prevent a civil establishment of the Roman Church in Ireland he pleaded for the abolishment of all establishments.[61] With his sermon he introduced a controversy, which lasted for the rest of the nineteenth century. The argument of Voluntaryism was that no church should be established or endowed by the law of the land, and that all religion should be supported by the free-will offerings of their members. The chief attack of the Voluntary Movement was against the endowments of the Church of Scotland. The Annuity Tax of Edinburgh from which the city ministers derived their stipend was an easy target.[62] So also was the attempt of Thomas Chalmers, in 1834, to obtain state endowed stipends for the ministers settled in the newly erected churches under his successful Church Extention Scheme. The Voluntaries succeeded in getting the government to drop this proposal for endowment.[63] The defenders of the Established Church tended to embrace the ideal of the Christian commonwealth against the

---

[58] Cunningham, 1822, ii.449; Hamilton, 1990:9
[59] Cunningham, 1822, ii.449
[60] Campbell, 1930:208
[61] Campbell, 1930:208
[62] Campbell, 1930:211
[63] Campbell, 1930:215

Voluntaries' liberal ideal of a pluralistic society of competing religious, social and economic interests.[64]

One effect of the Voluntary Controversy, which tore friendships and missionary and philanthropic societies apart, was renewed emphasis on the abolition of patronage within the Church of Scotland itself.[65] This led to a major confrontation between the Evangelicals in the General Assembly and the civil authority. On legal advice it was decided to introduce a law which would give to the majority of male heads in a parish who were in full communion with the Church of Scotland, the right to veto an unpopular presentation. The civil authorities, however, rejected the negative vote of the Evangelical Veto Act of the 1834 General Assembly as having no legal foundation.[66] The Evangelicals, or Non-Intrusionists as they came to be called, were unable to accept the verdict of the courts. They pleaded in the courts their conviction that the Church was a historical spiritual creation, recognised by statute, but with its own independent existence and sphere of jurisdiction. The courts, in turn, presented their theory of the Church's constitution: "that the Church was a creation of statute, subordinate to the legislature and the courts, having no independent jurisdiction."[67] The Moderates within the Church were willing to accept this theory but the Non-Intrusionists believed that to do so would compromise their belief in the Headship of Christ.[68]

Another Evangelical Act of the General Assembly brought further conflict between the Non-Intrusionists and the civil authorities. According to the Chapels Act of 1834 the General Assembly admitted ministers and elders from *quoad sacra* charges to the courts of the Church. All chapels-of-ease were previously unrepresented in church courts and were considered preaching stations of the parish churches. With the Chapels Act they were considered parish churches in the Scottish Establishment and were allowed to have kirk-sessions with disciplinary authority.[69] The Court of Session, however, found this Act incompetent,

---

[64] Brown, 1982:222
[65] Brown, 1982:223
[66] Brown, 1987:32
[67] Ross, 1988:5
[68] Ross, 1988:5
[69] Brown, 1982:234

and thus deprived some two hundred ministers of their seats in Presbyteries and Assemblies.[70]

Parliament's repeated refusal to pass modifying enactment, and the government's rejection in 1842 of an Evangelical "Claim of Right" to spiritual independence, led to secession. On 18 May 1843 the Evangelical Party walked out of the General Assembly in what was called the Disruption. Approximately 38 per cent of the ministers and possibly 40 per cent of the adherents left and constituted the Free Church of Scotland.[71] The intention was that never again would the spiritual independence of the church be called into question.[72] They held, however, to the establishment principle.

The Evangelicals held on to the principle of establishment, but in opposition to the state, they considered the church to be an institution with constituted laws and inherent authority to govern itself. In this continued controversy with its emphasis on the spiritual independence of the church over against the state, it was the Evangelicals who sharpened the Scottish ecclesiological conception of the church as an institution in terms of the universal church, and contributed to the bureaucratisation of the church.[73] In this respect the Voluntary controversy would be a constant support. The Headship of Christ was witnessed to, but the rule of the church was firmly in the hands of offices in assembly.

Within the Church of Scotland, patronage was abolished by law in 1874. With the rights of the local congregation restored, the road to reunion was opened. Different issues, however, came into play which led to the erosion of the Westminster Confession and which would require the disestablishment of the Church of Scotland. The purpose was Scottish Presbyterian reunion based on the principle of spiritual independence from the state.

---

[70] Ross, 1988:6
[71] Brown, 1987:32
[72] Ross, 1988:6
[73] Drummond and Bulloch, 1975:21

4.3 Bannerman, Macpherson and MacPhail

Views of evangelical writers confirmed the understanding of the church as an institution in terms of the universal church, and pointed out its connection with episcopalianism. Bannerman concerned himself with a systematic ecclesiology. His two volume work, *The Church of Christ,* was published by his son in 1868.

Unique in the work of Bannerman, in terms of Scottish presbyterian ecclesiology, was his strong insistence on the direct rule of Christ in His church. He maintained that "it is Christ in person, and by his actual presence in the Church" who still governs the church.[74] But he did not retain this strong emphasis on the direct rule of Christ throughout his consideration of the government of the church. In accordance with traditional Scottish presbyterian ecclesiology he held on to the assumption that the church was an institution representing the universal church. He considered it a "visible society" which has its origins in Christ,[75] and which was a "spiriual institution," or a "spiritual instrumentality for working out the spiritual good of men."[76] To this visible church an outward government was establishedfor the "order and regulation of the society of the elect."[77] He regarded the visible church as "one and universal, embracing all and uniting all, and the many local Churches, severed far and wide from each other, were merged and combined into the one catholic Church of the Saviour."[78]

Office-bearers were conceived by Bannerman to be office-bearers of the whole visible community of believers: "Both members and office-bearers stand related, in the first instance, to the Church catholic or universal, and only, in the second instance, to the Church local or particular."[79] Office-bearers and laws, "in other words a general power for government, and order, and action in the society of some sort" were essential.[80] Office-bearers were ordained and ordinances established with the purpose of "promoting the well-being and edification of the

---

[74] Bannerman, 1868a:206.
[75] Bannerman, 1868a:18.
[76] Bannerman, 1868a:23
[77] Bannerman, 1868a:30
[78] Bannerman, 1868a:35
[79] Bannerman, 1868a:47
[80] Bannerman, 1868a:188

Church."[81] It was from Christ that the church derived its government and office-bearers and it "receives from him its law and constitution."[82] Yet, "the church must be left very much to its own discretion in the framing of its constitution and the enactment of its laws," as long as it was subject to the authority of the Bible.[83] Like any other society the church needed "officers of some kind", a ministry "for the purpose of acting on behalf of the society and managing its affairs, more especially for conducting the stated and ordinary worship of the Church."[84] The "courts" were also considered by him to be expressive of the church as institution.[85]

Macpherson, also from the Free Church of Scotland, writing during the early eighteen eighties, considered presbyterianism to be an ecclesiastical system. He separated church government from doctrine.[86] His view on presbyterian church government reflects a consistent compromise with episcopacy. According to him, presbyterianism was a parochial instead of a diocesan episcopate.[87] The difference, "in general terms," was related to the parties entrusted with church power.[88] He considered the preaching of the Gospel to be basic and entrusted to the highest office.[89] The government and discipline of the church was to be conducted by the membership of the church through the elders ordained to rule.[90] The elders who held this position were the representatives of the people, though he recognised they may be accountable to some other authority: "as office-bearers discharging the functions of an office,

---

[81] Bannerman, 1868a:58
[82] Bannerman, 1868a:194
[83] Bannerman, 1868a:218
[84] Bannerman, 1868a:422
[85] Bannerman, 1868b:315; Brown, 1991:704
[86] Macpherson, [1883]:4-5; cf. Macphail, 1908:33-35
[87] Macpherson, [1883]:1 His book *Presbyterianism. Handbooks for Bible Classes* was reprinted in 1949 for the eighth time (van 't Spijker, 1990:327).
[88] Macpherson, [1883]:3. According to him ([1883]:3) in prelatical church government it is the clergy who rule, in Congregationalism the people and in Presbyterianism the representatives of the people in church courts variously graded, having their membership drawn from both the "clergy and the lay element."
[89] Macpherson, [1883]:7
[90] Macpherson, [1883]:8

they are not mere delegates of the people."[91] The oneness of the church remained basic and was, according to him, expressed by the fellowship of the church courts. He considered the constitution of the presbytery in this system as absolutely necessary.[92] A plurality of presbyteries must be brought into unity by association and combination in the synod as a superior court, having supervision over both the session and the presbytery.[93] Qualification for membership to the church courts was holding the office of presbyter.[94] The function of these courts was legislative, executive and judicial.[95] In the gradation of courts, the control of the higher courts over the lower courts was authoritative and not merely advisory.[96] The representative principle in presbyterianism, according to him, ensured the doctrine of the unity of the church.[97] The General Assembly is the "highest court in the Presbyterian Church and is representative of the whole church whose name it bears."[98] The church was understood by him to be a fellowship of believers and the aim of the church as institution was "the development of the fellowship of believers with Him who is the object of their faith." In this way he considered the Church of God and the Kingdom of Christ to be identical.[99] Since the kingdom "is within those who are members," the church meant "nothing else than the membership of the Church, and in each of its members Christ dwells by His Spirit, and over each He rules as Shepherd and King."[100] His conclusion was that in matters of church organization and government

> Presbyterianism is the constitutionalism which at the same time recognizes popular rights, assigning the rights of church power to the whole church, and conserves these rights for the

---

[91] Macpherson, [1883]:8
[92] Macpherson, [1883]:8
[93] Macpherson, [1883]:8
[94] Macpherson, [1883]:105
[95] Macpherson, [1883]:103
[96] Macpherson, [1883]:121
[97] Macpherson, [1883]:131
[98] Macpherson, [1881]:146
[99] Macpherson, [1883]:15
[100] Macpherson, [1883]:16

adequate accomplishment of those ends for which they have been conferred.[101] He held on to the three offices of minister, elder and deacon. The bishop and presbyter, according to him, were one and the same office. The office of presbyter included both the ruling and the teaching elders.[102] It was a mere wrangle over names whether to call both the elder and the minister a presbyter, or whether to "call the one a Teaching and the other a Ruling Presbyter."[103] Yet he maintained that preaching the gospel was a function of the "highest" office.[104]

According to Macphail, writing in 1908, presbyterianism was so called because it was the system that entrusted the rule of the church to presbyters.[105] Macphail emphasised the parity of the elders (ministerial and lay).[106] The representative system of government, according to him, enabled presbyterianism to express the unity of the church over a wide area.[107] He agreed that ministers were elected by congregations but stated that they held office by authority of the presbytery, and were accountable to the presbytery alone for the discharge of their duties.[108] He also maintained the connection between presbytery and episcopacy. Presbyterianism, according to him, substituted the hierarchy of solitary rule with a hierarchy of councils, with the right to appeal from a lower to a higher court.[109] The General Assembly was the supreme court and the final court of appeal. The congregation was considered part of the "greater whole" and by means of a gradation of representative courts presbyterianism extended the government of the church by its elders

---

[101]   Macpherson, [1883]:19
[102]   Macpherson, [1883]:35-36
[103]   Macpherson, [1883]:36
[104]   Macpherson, [1883]:7
[105]   Macphail, 1908:127; Burleigh (1949:298) maintained that presbyterianism means government by presbyteries.
[106]   Macphail, 1908:129
[107]   Macphail, 1908:130
[108]   Macphail, 1908:131
[109]   Macphail, 1908:138

over as wide an area as possible.[110] In this regard, he held that presbyterianism and episcopacy "are at one in principle."[111]

4.4 The church in the process of Presbyterian reunion

The ecclesiological premise of the church as institution in terms of the universal church compelled Scottish presbyterianism to take the question of presbyterian reunion into consideration. In this process a major concern was the spiritual independence of the church. This raised the question of the relationship between church and state and, consequently, the question of the church's relation to its confessional standard. In the process of presbyterian reunion, two opposing viewpoints could be discerned. On the one side there were those who held to the Calvinism of the Westminster Confession of Faith and the principle of national establishment. On the other side there were those, the majority, who approved of a departure from the Scottish Church's historical attachment to its confessional standard, discarded the principle of national establishment and favoured presbyterian reunion.

The Westminster Confession acknowledged the role of the civil magistrate in spiritual matters.[112] Act X of the General Assembly of the Church of Scotland of 1711 required ministers and probationers to "own and believe the whole doctrine contained in the Confession of Faith ... to be the truths of God" and to "own the same *as the confession of my faith*."[113] The churches of the secession, including the Relief Church, originally held to this formula of subscription.[114] It was, however, within these circles that the first relaxation of subscription according to the 1711 Act was enacted. This related initially to the role of the civil magistrate in the church. As already mentioned, those churches that united in 1820 to form the United Secession Church took with them the new conviction of disestablishment by denying the civil magistrate any role in the church. In addition, the United Secession Church's relation to the Westminster Confession of Faith was expressed as "we retain the Westminster Con-

---

[110] Macphail, 1908:212
[111] Macphail, 1908:212
[112] WCF, XX.4; XXX; XXXI.2, 5
[113] AGA 1638-1842:456. Italics mine
[114] Hamilton, 1990:10, 20

fession of Faith, as the confession of our faith, *expressive of the sense in which we understand the Holy Scripture*."[115] Those unhappy with what they considered to be a change in theological emphasis in the new United Secession Church seceded and joined with the remnant of the Old Light Anti-Burghers to form the Associate Synod of Original Seceders.[116]

In 1823 the Relief Church followed the United Secession Church by modifying its relation to the Westminster Confession with regard to the role of the civil magistrate in the church.[117] These two churches united in 1847 to form the United Presbyterian Church. By this time more that just the relationship between the church and state influenced these churches' departure from their historical attachment to the Westminster Confession. Theological issues came into view. The Atonement Controversy, which lasted from 1841 until 1845 in the United Secession Church, resulted in a breach between those convinced that the Westminster doctrine held a limited atonement and those who now taught a general and universal atonement.[118] Against this background the United Presbyterian Church moved to a position in which the Westminster Standards were no longer held on the same high level as they were held by other presbyterian churches in Scotland.[119] Continued theological controversy in the United Presbyterian Church led to the passing of declaratory legislation in 1879 aimed at allowing its ministers personal liberty of opinion in matters, which did not enter "the substance of faith."[120]

The Free Church left the Established Church because of the interference of the civil courts in matters spiritual, but held on to the establishment principle, convinced that they were not Voluntaries.[121]

In addition, this church held an "unyielding and enthusiastic loyalty to Westminster Calvinism."[122] But both the commitment to Westminster

---

[115] As quoted by Hamilton, 1990:16. Italics mine
[116] Hamilton, 1990:17
[117] Hamilton, 1990:20, 23
[118] Hamilton, 1990:24, 38, 74
[119] Hamilton, 1990:24
[120] Hamilton, 1990:24
[121] Brown, 1982:337

Calvinism and the establishment principle were subject to change and received attention in the 1863-1873 union discussion with the United Presbyterian Church. Contrary to the Free Church of Scotland, the United Presbyterian Church was in the forefront against establishment and was considered to hold an unsound "Amyraldian" theory on atonement. The passage of time, however, made each aware of how much they held in common and the presbyterian unions in the colonies apparently influenced moves toward union.[123] In 1863 the question of union was taken up formally by the two Churches. These ten years saw an intense struggle between the Unionists and Anti-Unionists in the Free Church of Scotland on the question of union with the United Presbyterian Church. A major issue was the question of establishment and voluntaryism. When Robert Buchanan introduced the motion to seek union with the United Presbyterian Church at the Free Church Assembly in 1863, he and Charles Brown - two of the Church's most senior ministers - argued that establishment had become an academic question: "We have now no State endowments. We do not expect any. We don't desire any."[124] In addition Buchanan argued that union would emphasise the Church's spiritual independence from the state, and better prosecute the evangelization of Scotland.[125] To a lesser extent, attention was paid to a subject of equal, if not greater, importance. This was the concern of the Anti-Unionists that the principles of the Free Church must be maintained in their integrity.[126] They were convinced that the United Presbyterian Church had departed substantially from the heritage of Westminster.[127] Union discussions were suspended in the early 1870s and were taken up again in 1894. By this time the theological change, which had occurred in the Free Church found expression in the Declaratory Act of 1892. Some seceded to form the Free Presbyterian Church. In agreement with the seceders the Anti-Unionists who remained in the Free Church, and who

---

[122] Ross, 1988:9
[123] Ross, 1982:15. Presbyterian unions took place in Victoria (1859), Nova Scotia (1860), Canada (1861), New Zealand (1862) and New South Wales (1865) (Ross, 1988:306).
[124] Ross, 1988:16
[125] Hamilton, 1990:89
[126] Ross, 1988:16
[127] Hamilton, 1990:89

were called the Constitutionalists in the union discussion which started in 1894, considered this Act a qualification of the confessional teaching and thus an alteration in the doctrinal position of the Church.[128] With this change in the attachment of the Free Church to its confession and with its strong commitment, under the leadership of Principal Rainy, to the Disestablishment campaign[129] during the last two decades of the nineteenth century, the way was opened for union with the United Presbyterian Church. The United Free Church was formed in 1900. The Constitutionalist minority in the Free Church of Scotland, however, maintained that the majority "may lawfully be held to have withdrawn from membership of the Free Church of Scotland."[130] They continued the Free Church in accordance with Free Church principles of establishment and a total commitment to the Westminster Confession of Faith.

Theological changes during the course of the nineteenth century affected the Church of Scotland as well. As early as 1865 the question of the elders' subscription to the Confession of Faith in accordance with the rigid formula of 1711 was raised. An Act of 1899 reverted to a milder formula of subscription for elders, but it was only in 1905 that full constitutional relief was obtained for ministers of this Church.[131] By a Parliamentary Act of 1874 patronage was abolished in the Church of Scotland. Those behind this action in the Establishment promoted it with a view to reunification of Scottish presbyterianism.[132] This unilateral action, however, resulted in a vigorous Disestablishment campaign on the side of the Unionists in the Free Church and the United Presbyterian Church. The firm conviction was that union was only possible on a footing of independence from the state.[133] Despite the adoption of an act "Anent Spiritual Independence" in 1906 by the United Free Church of Scotland, discussions on union commenced with the Church of Scotland in November 1909. Convinced that no doctrinal issues kept the two

---

[128] Ross, 1988:29
[129] Fleming, 1927:238
[130] Ross, 1988:40
[131] Fleming, 1933:17
[132] Ross, 1988:120
[133] Ross, 1988:122, 124; Fleming, 1933:238

churches apart, the major difficulties were considered to lie in the areas of spiritual independence and establishment.[134] With the legal obstacles removed by a parliamentary act of 1921, a comprehensive Scottish presbyterian reunion was achieved in 1929.

The Westminster Confession of Faith became an inadequate basis for unity in the Church of Scotland and the emphasis fell on the uniting of church institutions with their peculiar form of government. In this restructuring of Scottish presbyterianism the unity of the Church was considered from the premise of the universal church. This was a premise that would be followed in twentieth century ecumenical discussions, but it was an ecclesiological starting point that did not allow for a theological consideration and development of the ministry of the reformed offices.

The one-sided presbyterian emphasis on the church as institution as departure point for theological reflection on the government of the visible church is reflected in an official statement of the Church of Scotland, prepared in the process of reunion with the then United Free Church of Scotland. According to the *Articles Declaratory of the Constitution of the Church of Scotland in matters spiritual, passed by Parliament, 1921; and enacted by General Assembly, 1926,* the government of the Church of Scotland was presbyterian, and was "exercised through Kirk-Sessions, Presbyteries, Provincial Synods and General Assemblies."[135] Furthermore, this church

> as part of the Universal Church wherein the Lord Jesus Christ has appointed a government *in the hands of Church office-bearers, receives from Him,* its divine King and from Him alone, *the right and power* subject to no civil authority to *legislate and to adjudicate finally,* in all matters of doctrine, worship, government, and discipline in the Church, *including the right to determine* all questions concerning membership and office in the church, the constitution and membership of its Courts, and the mode of election of its office-bearers, and to define the boundaries of the spheres of labour of its ministers and other office-bearers.[136]

---

134 Fleming, 1933:86
135 Fleming, 1933:310
136 Fleming, 1933:311. Italics mine

In addition it was stated that this church had

> the inherent right, free from interference by civil authority, but under the safeguards for deliberate action and legislation *provided by the Church itself*, to frame or adopt its subordinate standards, to declare the sense in which it understands its Confession of Faith, to modify the forms of expression therein, or to formulate other doctrinal statements, and to define the relation thereto of its office-bearers and members, but always in agreement with the Word of God and the fundamental doctrines of the Christian faith contained in the said Confession, of which agreement the Church shall be the sole judge.[137]

It has been suggested that Scottish theology was "so woefully weak in respect of the concept of the Church as body of Christ that the Church was thought of as no more divine than any man-made association."[138] In this approach to church government no room was left for the development of the reformed offices as ministries serving the direct rule of Christ through His Word and Spirit.

---

[137] Fleming, 1933:311. Italics mine. Three nagging questions, however, remain: a) what is considered to be the Word of God? b) what are the fundamental doctrines of the Christian Faith contained in the said Confession? c) Who determines what they are?

[138] Donaldson, 1990:116

CHAPTER 5

THE TEACHING AND RULING ELDERS

UNLIKE THE PRESBYTERIAL-SYNODICAL FORM OF CHURCH GOVERNMENT THE Scottish presbyterian tradition did not maintain parity of the offices of minister, elder and deacon. The office of minister received a special position in comparison with that of the other offices. It was considered the highest position in the church.

The office of elder continued to be an accepted office but questions centred on its position and function. The relationship between the teaching and ruling elder was explored in terms of "presbyter" and "lay" theories. Considered an official of the church the elder was relegated to a position secondary to that of the minister of the Word and sacraments. The understanding of the elder as an assistant to the minister prevented the development of this office as a ministry in its own right.

5.1 The minister

Both social factors and theological considerations distinguished the office of minister as the highest office. Its introduction to Scotland represented a radical challenge to the social and political context. It was realised that the full implementation of the provisos of the *First Book of Discipline* would have brought about a virtual social revolution in Scotland. The power of the burgesses and lairds to appoint ministers and elders would have been placed in the hands of ministers and elders.[1] Despite the fact that the provisions of this *First Book of Discipline* and the theocracy of the *Second Book of Discipline* were never fully implemented, the minister held a vital position between the patron and the people - between royal absolutism and the spiritual independence of the church. With the additional emphasis on a highly trained ministry and the "dignity of a

---

[1] cf. Reid, 1982:206-207

divine calling,"[2] the position and influence of the minister in religious, social and political affairs were certain. Considered "an Order of a definite kind," specific Scottish conditions served to "enable it the better to realize itself."[3] The extreme power wielded by ministers during the mid-seventeenth century rule of presbyterianism was replaced by an emphasis on cultural, intellectual and social attainment during the latter half of the eighteenth century.[4] The accompanying decay in spiritual and ministerial functions was countered by the development of an evangelical ministry as a result of evangelical revivals during the eighteenth and nineteenth centuries. Despite social and theological trends, people looked up to the minister for guidance in matters of principle, for advice in dilemmas, and for improvement in standard of living.[5] In general the commitment and leadership of ministers was reflected in their sermon preparation, responsibilities for relief of the poor, supervision of parish schools and frequent house visitation.

Since the time of the *Second Book of Discipline*, the minister had been formally differentiated from his congregation and the other offices. The Westminster *Forme of Presbyterian Church-Government* viewed the office of minister as a distinct clerical office. The superiority of the office of minister to that of the elder and deacon was maintained in the Scottish Church.[6] The conviction was that the ministry of the Word and sacraments belonged to the "highest" office.[7] In the same way pronouncement of excommunication was the prerogative of the minister.

The importance of the ministerial office as a distinct office is reflected in the understanding of the minister's relationship to the congregation. The minister was elected by the congregation but held the office by the authority of the presbytery and was accountable to the presbytery alone for the discharge of his duties.[8] One of the questions, which James VI

---

[2] Henderson, 1951a:17
[3] Ainslee, 1940:15
[4] Mackie, 1966:299-300; Chitnis, 1976:34
[5] Glover, 1960:276
[6] cf. the Form of Process, AGA 1638-1842:405 and the Extracts from the "Theological Institutes" of George Hill in Compendium, Part 1.445.
[7] Macpherson, [1883]:7; Torrance, 1958:247
[8] cf. Extracts Hill, Compendium, Part 1.445; MacPhail, 1908:131

put forward at the meeting of the Perth Assembly of 1597 was: "Is not his sessioun judge to his [the minister's] doctrine?" Replies were given by the Synod of Fife, Patrick Gordon of Galloway, and by "Another Brother." The reply from the Synod of Fife was that only pastors and doctors could be judges of ministers. The reply from Patrick Gordon was a straightforward "no".[9] The "Other Brother" replied:

reference to an act of the Parliament of King William and Queen Mary, Steuart of Pardovan pointed out:

> it is to be remembered, that no probationer or minister, could receive any call to a vacant congregation, but from the hands of the Presbytery to which they belong: For it is by their determination that the calling and entry of a minister is to be ordered and concluded.[10]

Ordination was considered a solemn act of the presbytery. According to Principal Hill

> the office of the minister being superior to that of an elder, and the minister of a parish being officially the moderator of his own kirk-session, he is not amenable to their jurisdiction. His immediate superiors are the presbytery from where he received the charge of his parish.[11]

This conviction was held onto by the different presbyterian churches during the nineteenth century. The view was that "all processes against any minister, who hath charge of a congregation are to begin before the presbytery to which he belongeth, and not before the kirk-session of his parish." [12] According to Cox,[13] writing in the twentieth century, elders were under the jurisdiction of the kirk session but the minister

> is not responsible to the Kirk Session for the discharge of his ministerial functions; but, if he seems to neglect these, or to

---

[9] Foster, 1975:88
[10] Compendium, Part 1.178
[11] Compendium, Part 1:445
[12] AGA 1638-1842:411; Form of Process in Compendium, Part 1.156. cf. the Relief Church, Struthers, 1943:278; Rules and Forms UPC, 1869:21f.f; Forbes' Digest FCS, 1869:60
[13] Cox, 1934:102

encroach upon the functions of the Kirk Session, the Presbytery may be approached by petition.[14]

The specific position of the minister was underlined by the repeated emphasis that the church allowed no power in the people, but only in the pastors of the church, to appoint and ordain church officers.[15] This conviction was maintained even in those churches where the relationship between the minister and elder reflected the least distinction in rank and dignity. The proposal, for example, that a ruling elder may participate in the ordination of the teaching elder was rejected by the Synod of the United Presbyterian Church of May 1851.[16]

The minister's distinct position from the other offices was emphasised with reference to the question of moderatorship of church assemblies. Practice and law, for example, required the minister to be ex officio moderator of the kirk session.[17] Without the presence of a minister as moderator no meeting of a church court could be held.[18] The Panel on Doctrine, a committee of the General Assembly of the Church of Scotland, rejected the assumption of the report on Conversations with the Congregational Union of Scotland presented to the General Assembly of 1962, that "there is nothing in the law of the church of Scotland to prevent a layman being Moderator of the General Assembly." The Panel referred to Steuart of Pardovan who wrote that only a minister can be a moderator of the kirk session, and also to an Act of 1944 of the General Assembly that only a minister could be moderator of a presbytery. The panel's conclusion was that "since it is the law that a minister is required to moderate in these lower Courts, the Panel does not see how this could be invalidated in the case of the Supreme Court." Fleming referred to the "pride in place" of the moderator of the General

---

[14] Cox, 1934:104
[15] cf. Act 5 of Assembly, 1698, Compendium, Part 1:185; Pardovan's Collection, Compendium, Part 1:180; Scottish Church Society, 1927:5; and the reaction of the Panel on Doctrine to the report on the Conversations with the Congregational Union of Scotland (Report, 1963:749).
[16] Proceedings UPC, 1847-1856:314
[17] Rules and Forms UPC, 1883:1; Forbes' Digest FCS, 1869:32; Cox, 1934:103
[18] Forbes' Digest, 1869:32, 53; Cox, 1934:103. Report, 1963:749-750.

Assembly.[19] Highet, though, warned against a wrong conception of the moderator of the General Assembly:

He is the Moderator of the General Assembly of the Church of Scotland and not of the Church of Scotland. He cannot make pronouncement on behalf of the Church of Scotland outwith decisions of the General Assembly.[20]

More exalted claims for the office of the minister were made within the circle of the so-called Scoto-Catholics, represented mainly within the Scottish Church Society, founded in 1892. Their approach to the church and its offices represented an ecclesiasticism and clericalism in an episcopal sense. They considered the church "a divine organization for administering grace and carrying out God's eternal purpose,"[21] and

> a society of individuals owning the authority of Christ and the value of the Gospel, who associate themselves together, that in acts of common worship and of ministerial edification they may strengthen and comfort one another in their religious life.[22]

In this context, according to Sprott, "a rightly constituted ministry is essential to the proper existence of the Church."[23]

A twofold order of bishop and deacon was held onto. The bishop and presbyter were considered to be one and the same. The "presbyterate" was considered the "highest" and fundamental order, which did not include reference to the reformation elder.[24] In a document titled *Presbyterian Orders,* published by the Scottish Church Society in 1926 it was stated that "right Presbyterian courts are those that are composed of right Presbyterian office-bearers."[25] Presbyterianism, according to this document, is government by presbyters, not presbyteries,[26] "but presbyters as distinguished from prelates."[27] Convinced of the presbyter

---

[19] Fleming, 1933:206
[20] Hieght, 1960;19
[21] Sprott, 1877:7
[22] Milligan, 1895:8. Italics mine.
[23] Sprott, 1877:9
[24] Sprott, 1882:188; Wotherspoon, 1909:19; Wotherspoon and Kirkpatrick, [1920]:158-159
[25] *Presbyterian Orders*, 1927:4
[26] Wotherspoon, 1909:19; Leishman, 1909:52
[27] *Presbyterian Orders*, 1927:4

as the foundation of presbyterianism, the document continued that the present government "rests upon the authority inherent in the Ministerial office as this was exercised by a certain number of presbyters." For this reason "the qualifications of the ministers of a religious community are of vital importance to the validity of its government."[28] This touches upon the question of a valid ordination.

> For a minister to establish his credentials as a minister he had to prove that he had been ordained by those who themselves were ministers of the Word and Sacrament. A "presbyterian" view of apostolic succession was presented. The conviction was that the principle of 'commission at the hands of the commissioned' leaves, on a fair interpretation, no intermediate stopping place short of the first depositories of the commission, the Apostles who received from Jesus Christ himself.[29]

According to this document the Church of Scotland followed to its logical conclusion their teaching that "commission to the Ministry can be given by the commissioned only, and they stand by the doctrine of Apostolic Succession."[30]

That the *First Book of Discipline* considered the "laying on of hands" unnecessary in the admission of ministers to their offices was a matter of great offence to those holding the apostolic succession and valid ordination view on the office of the minister. *Presbyterian Orders* described the *First Book of Discipline* as a draft, which did not possess the authority of the church and had never been adopted by the General Assembly.[31] Story considered it "an abrupt departure from Apostolic usage"[32] and Sprott, because of this omission tried to discredit this discipline.[33] Wotherspoon considered it a book of no consequence.[34] The authors of the document *Presbyterian Orders* were adamant in pointing out that a system is presbyterian when a true doctrine of the

---

[28] *Presbyterian Orders*, 1927:5
[29] *Presbyterian Orders*, 1927:8.
[30] *Presbyterian Orders*, 1927:9
[31] *Presbyterian Orders*, 1927:11
[32] Story, 1897:245-246
[33] Ainslee, 1940:170
[34] Wotherspoon, 1909:22-23

Holy Ministry is "both confessed and uniformly acted upon."[35] A plea was made for the church to safeguard this gift. And an appeal was made to "Presbyters to maintain their own Orders."[36]

Those subscribing to the doctrine of apostolic succession were in agreement with the statement *of Jus Divinum Ministerii Evangelici*, published in 1654 in London: "Ordination, in the view of our Church makes a minister, as Baptism makes him a members of God's Church."[37] This approach to the office of the minister was held onto by TF Torrance in the twentieth century. He maintained that the order of presbyterial ministry is not only the highest order but in the strict sense the only order of the ministry. Other "so-called" orders were either for the "assistance of this order or for convenience of maintaining the unity and concord and discipline among those so ordained."[38] He attempted to make this view acceptable to the General Assembly of the Church of Scotland.

5.2 The eldership: an overview

In the period of the Covenants of the mid-seventeenth century it was suggested that "the Eldership of the Church was most efficient and powerful."[39] Emphasis was on strict and comprehensive discipline, religious education of the elderly and the young, and instruction and examination with a view to participation in the Lord's Supper.[40] A notable tract, called *A Treatise of Ruling Elders and Deacons*, generally attributed to James Guthrie,[41] was published during this period "to spur on the Eldership to what the Lord doth require them to do."[42] Contrary to the divines of the Westminster Assembly, the author was more interested in providing useful information to motivate and assist the elder in his duties rather than in a polemical affirmation of the office of elder. He

---

[35] *Presbyterian Orders*, 1927:15
[36] *Presbyterian Orders*, 1927:16
[37] Leishman, 1909:54; Wotherspoon, 1909:39; Wright, 1895:175
[38] Torrance, 1958:247
[39] Lorimer, 1842a:xiv
[40] Hill, 1919:179; Lorimer, 1842a:140, 150, 151
[41] First published in 1652 it was reprinted by order of the General Assembly of the Church of Scotland after establishment of Presbyterianism in 1690.
[42] Lorimer, 1842a:xxvi; A copy was published in both the 1841 and 1842 editions of *The Eldership of the Church of Scotland*, by GD Lorimer.

distinguished the four offices of teaching elder, preaching elder, ruling elder, and deacon. In addition, he pointed out two mistakes that needed to be avoided. The first mistake was to call ruling elders "lay" elders, "as if they were part of the people only, and not to be reckoned amongst the officers of the Lord's house." For this reason the distinction "clergy" and "laity" was also to be rejected. The second mistake to avoid was to call the elder attending presbytery, synod and general assembly meetings, the "ruling" elder. According to him "every Elder in the Lord's house is a ruling Elder."[43] He maintained the divine institution of the elder and believed that 1 Tim 5:17 referred to two kinds of elders: one who laboured in Word and doctrine and another who only ruled.[44] He laid down a comprehensive list of the duties of elders; some personal which touched upon his character and moral behaviour, others official which were public; some private as a fellow believer and overseer in the community, and others public with reference to attendance at the courts of the church.[45] He recommended that one elder from every session attend presbytery and synod meetings, and that a few from the presbytery attend the General Assembly.[46] Concerning the election of elders he recommended that this be done by the congregation. The best way to do this, according to him, was for the minister and the session to make a list to be presented to the congregation who could then add to it or present objections.[47]

One of the few changes made in the period after the Restoration was the exclusion of elders from the presbytery meetings.[48] The elders appeared to have being elected by and been active in local congregations during the period of episcopal reign between 1660 to 1888.[49]

---

[44] Lorimer, 1842a:28
[44] Lorimer, 1842a:28-32
[45] Lorimer, 1842a:34-42
[46] Lorimer, 1842a:42
[47] Lorimer, 1842a:33
[48] Foster, 1957:72
[49] Lorimer, 1842a:141

There may have been an increase in the elders' activities after the establishment of presbyterianism in 1690.[50] It would seem, however, that the qualification and function of the elder was a grave concern and received the attention of the General Assembly from time to time. In 1697 it was enacted that "none be made ruling elders who make not conscience of family worship."[51] In May 1722, an act Against Profanes and the Duties of Elders and Deacons was accepted. An appeal was made to ministers and elders to take heed of themselves in the light of

> the great decay of Christian piety amongst all ranks, and the abounding vice and immorality, the neglect of public ordinances, and profanation of the Lord's Day; and considering that slackness and particularly in the exercise of discipline, and untenderness in the work and conversation of the office-bearers of this Church, cannot but greatly contribute to the increase of these evils.[52]

Reference was made to this Act in 1724, 1727 and 1737 in connection with the qualifications of elders attending the General Assembly.[53]

A very bleak picture, however, is painted of the eldership in terms of quality and availability throughout the eighteenth century.[54] This was contrary to the apparently much more effective eldership in the secession churches.[55] It was suggested that under the reign of the Moderates, during the second half of the eighteenth century, the spiritual function of the ruling elder was lost sight of, and attention to outward parochial affairs was regarded as exhaustive of the duties of the local church session.[56] The decay in the eldership seems to have been part of a general decay in church life during this period. From mid-1790 there was an insistent outcry against poor church attendance.[57] A pamphlet in

---

[50] Lorimer, 1842a:153, 155
[51] AGA 1638-1842:259
[52] AGA 1638-1842:559
[53] AGA 1638-1942:569, 588, 645
[54] It is possible to come to this conclusion also concerning the first decade of the eighteenth century, cf. *Collections and Observations* of Steuart of Pardovan (Compendium, Part 1.208, §2).
[55] Henderson, 1935:176; Fleming, 1933:117
[56] Macpherson, [1883]:64
[57] Withrington, 1972:104; Henderson, 1935:229

1806 dealt with the effect of the state of the established Church's kirk sessions and with a "terrible weakness" found in the local eldership. On the local church level it was complained that members of the church were no longer instructed and catechised as they ought to have been, the preparation preceding communion had ceased, and "now tokens were merely given out to gentlemen, masters, and manufacturers for them to distribute among their servants, dependants and neighbours."[58] On the higher court level things did not appear to have been any better.

The concept of the "ruling elder" as the one to attend higher courts was still held to in the early nineteenth century[59] despite Guthrie's objection. The parish elders were considered to be concerned with matters on the local church council level, while the "ruling" elders, "the most qualified noblemen, gentlemen and burgesses" that the area could "afford", as Robert Baillie put it, sat in the higher courts of the church.[60] The position of ruling elder, initially held mainly by higher classes, was by the nineteenth century filled mostly with lawyers from Edinburgh. It was reported that in the Assembly of 1820 72 out of 133 elders were lawyers (including nine judges).[61] Wrong motives for attending the General Assembly were not always absent.[62] During the second half of the eighteenth century a practice developed in which elders would seek appointment to the General Assembly through a local parish without necessarily residing in that parish. An attempt in 1784 to curb this practice and to send only elders who had fixed residence in their congregations failed.[63] The General Assembly of May 1816 confirmed the practice, stating that elders elected to the General Assembly ought to

---

[58] Withrington, 1972:109; It is still a practice today (1995) in Presbyterian and Reformed Churches in Central Africa that "tokens" are handed to those attending the Saturday preparation service for Holy Communion. Without these a person is not allowed to attend Holy Communion the next day.
[59] Withrington, 1972:110; *Presbyterian Review*, November 1834:31; Henderson (1935:168) mentioned that this distinction was still found in the 1930s with this elder given a special place at Communion and at session meetings.
[60] Maciver, 1980:1
[61] Maciver, 1980:2; Drummond and Bullock, 1973:43
[62] Maciver, 1980:3-5
[63] AGA 1638-1842:821-822

be at least twenty-one years of age, and if not a heritor, or heir apparent to the heritor, they must reside for at least six weeks annually in that parish through which they received appointment.[64]

It has been suggested that in the Church of Scotland in those days the office might have died out altogether had it not been essential for holding a seat in the General Assembly.[65] Elders were scarce. An inquiry by the General Assembly in 1817 and again in the 1830s confirmed that the eldership was weak in numbers.[66] This was pointed out in an article in the November 1834 issue of the Presbyterian Review, an Edinburgh periodical and mouth piece of the younger and more radical Evangelicals in the Church.[67] According to the writer, understood to be Alexander Dunlop, advocate and elder of the Church of Scotland, several parishes had no elders, one elder in a congregation was not uncommon, and sessions with only two elders were numerous in some parts of the country.[68] Dunlop referred to returns from presbyteries on this point, ordered by the General Assembly of 1828, from which it appeared that the average number of elders to each session throughout Scotland could not possibly have exceeded four and probably not more than three.[69] In the *Presbyterian Review* of January 1835 he pointed out three causes for the deterioration of the eldership. The first was the practice of ordaining elders who were not intended to perform any of the proper functions of the office, but merely in order to qualify them for sitting in the General Assembly.[70] The second cause was the practice of the intrusion of ministers into parishes against the wishes of the people which resulted in elders leaving the Church of Scotland and joining seceding churches.[71] The third cause of deterioration was considered to be the mode of election. The writer complained that the contemporary practice placed nomination and election of elders in the session without the necessity even of the consent of the people, and at times it even

---

[64] AGA 1638-1842:952;
[65] Henderson, 1935:229; Dicksen, 1871:4
[66] Donald, 1990:40
[67] Maciver, 1980:8
[68] *Presbyterian Review*, November, 1834:31
[69] *Presbyterian Review*, November, 1834:31
[70] *Presbyterian Review*, January, 1835:166
[71] *Presbyterian Review*, January, 1835:167

happened that they were ordained in the session-house without the presence of the people altogether.[72] Both Lorimer and M'Kerrow, writing on the eldership in the 1840s, complained about an ineffective eldership.[73]

The practice of ordaining elders for the purpose of attending the General Assembly, synod or presbytery was stopped by an Act of the General Assembly in 1839. The Act required that elders attending the higher courts had to produce a certificate from their sessions indicating that they were indeed bona fide resident elders in their congregations.[74] Thomas Chalmers, however, motivated by the poverty in the growing industrialised Glasgow, commenced in 1816 with an experiment in urban ministry.[75] Convinced of the advantages of the parochial system which seems to have been neglected in the cities, he divided the Tron parish, the poorest and most violent in the city, into small districts and began visiting each and every family. He introduced elders who had to go on regular house-to-house visitation. They were required to communicate Christian knowledge and consolation to the inhabitants, help the poor, and encourage wealthier families to help those in temporary distress. At the same time he started Sabbath school classes in each district and commenced parish schools.[76] Greater participation in the election of elders by the congregations was provided for in an Act of the General Assembly of 1842, which was repealed again in 1845, two years after the Disruption.[77] In the Free Church Chalmers' emphasis on the elder was adopted and an increase in the elders' activities were experienced. It was especially in this church and other secession churches that the eldership received attention. In terms of numbers, Dickson reported in 1871 that there were 6500 elders in the Free Church, 4250 in the United Presbyterian Church and 300 in the small Reformed Presbyterian Church.[78]

---

[72] *Presbyterian Review*, January, 1835:169
[73] Henderson, 1935:229
[74] AGA 1638-1842:1097
[75] Brown, 1982:99
[76] Brown, 1982: 101, 102, 103
[77] AGA 1638-1942:1125ff
[78] Dickson, 1871:2

Fleming held a favourable opinion of the early twentieth century elder. He wrote on the emergence of a new elder in all churches during the second half of the last century. This new elder was the "liberal giver, the devoted Sunday-school teacher, the earnest business man, the speaker who had gained proficiency in the law courts or in the Town Council."[79] In 1933 he wrote that the elder "was coming more and more to his own as a true presbyter, not merely 'admitted' but 'ordained'."[80]

G.D. Henderson, a Scottish church historian convinced of the lay character of the elder, in 1935 published a major work, *The Scottish Ruling Elder*. He pointed to the erosion of the functions of the eldership during the second half of the nineteenth century. The reasons he gave were poor relief and education taken over by the State, and discipline hardly exercised.[81] According to him, the emphasis had shifted more towards the spiritual functions and away from the more administrative functions of the elder.[82] As for the eldership of his own time, he stated that it had lost its significance and was in need of modification and exaltation.[83] At more or less the same time, considering the elder as layman,[84] Henderson, as president *of The Fellowship of Equal Service in the Church*, aiming at removal of the barriers to the eligibility of women for the ministry and the eldership, appealed for the admission of women to the eldership.[85] The eldership was opened to women in 1966.[86]

5.3 The elder: presbyter or layman

The eldership as a divine institution was challenged during the latter half of the nineteenth century search for improvement of the eldership. John Lorimer, an Evangelical of the pre-Disruption church, in *The Eldership of the Church of Scotland*, 1841, David King from the United Secession Church and later the United Presbyterian Church, *in The Ruling*

---

[79] Fleming, 1927:258
[80] Fleming, 1933:208
[81] Henderson, 1935:229
[82] Henderson, 1935:232
[83] Henderson, 1935:287
[84] Henderson, 1935:303
[85] Henderson, 1935:305; Henderson, G.D. n.d., *Women and the Eldership*.
[86] Report, 1966

Eldership of the Christian Church, 1844, and the prize winner,[87] John M'Kerrow also of the United Secession Church, in *The Office of the Ruling Elder in the Christian Church*, 1846, all argued for the divine institution of the elder even though they did not reach their conclusions in the same manner.

Lorimer rejected the reference to the elder as a "lay" elder and insisted that the correct term is "ruling elder" in distinction from "teaching elder."[88] Paying attention to the history of the elder and basing his argument on the New Testament arising out of the Old Testament, he stated that it was the Old Testament that provided the first proof for the presence of a ruling elder in the government of the church. It was very clear to him that the New Testament accepted this office in every church.[89] He found specific proof for the ruling elder in the following references: "he that ruleth" in Rom 12:6-8, the "governments" in 1 Cor 12:28, and the vital passage on the theory of the ruling elder, in 1 Tim 5:17. The last mentioned, he believed, clearly distinguished two classes of elders - those who ruled and those who laboured in Word and doctrine.[90] He complained that there had been a "vast expenditure of ingenuity to make the verse harmonise" with other theories.[91] Convinced that the elder was an ecclesiastical office, he understood the office to be an aid to the minister who needed assistance in the management, discipline and government of the congregation.[92]

According to King, there was one office of the presbyter with two parts, namely "teaching and ruling".[93] He emphasised that there were no

---

[87] A competition advertised "The Sum of Fifty Pounds Sterling is offered for the best Essay on the following subject The Scriptural Authority, Duties, and Responsibilities of the Office of "Ruling Elder" in the Christian Church. The Duties of the "Elder" and those of the "Deacon": to be clearly distinguished from each other" was won by John M'Kerrow (M'Kerrow, 1846:iv).
[88] Lorimer, 1842a:58-59
[89] Lorimer, 1842a:61-66
[90] Lorimer, 1842a:66-69
[91] Lorimer, 1842a:70
[92] Lorimer, 1842a:60, 61, 86, 87, 89
[93] King, 1846:51

lay elders, for all elders were spiritual office bearers.[94] The most decisive proof in favour of ruling elders he found in 1 Tim 5:17. He emphasised that all the office-bearers spoken of in this passage ruled: some of those who ruled were also public teachers. To all of them ample honour was due, and especially to the latter, who were "pre-eminently occupied."[95] In the revised edition of his work, King objected to those who based their proof of the office of ruling elder on grounds other than those with which he had been defending it.[96] M'Kerrow, in turn, maintained that there was no comparison made in 1 Tim 5:17 between those who ruled and those who did not rule. There was a comparison between the ruling of some, and the ruling of others.[97] There were none especially entitled to receive double honour because they laboured in Word and doctrine, but because they ruled.[98] The conclusion must therefore be drawn that besides the elders who ruled whether well or not, there was another group who ruled well and who laboured in Word and doctrine.[99] Like Lorimer he considered the elder an assistant to the minister.[100]

In describing the qualifications and duties of elders, the three authors, with contemporary needs in mind, followed the same broad outlines as those presented by Guthrie. A significant emphasis is found by Lorimer and King on district fellowship and prayer meeting.[101] Lorimer would, in addition, like to see the elder as Sunday School teacher in his district, a distributor of tracts and of missionary intelligence.[102]

Lorimer saw only advantages to the eldership in the new system of greater popular election approved by the General Assembly of 1842,[103] but he warned that it should never be so absolute as to exclude the concurrence of the existing session.[104] In the United Presbyterian

---

[94] King, 1846:52
[95] King, 1846:60
[96] King, 1846:60
[97] M'Kerrow, 1846:92
[98] M'Kerrow, 1846:94
[99] M'Kerrow, 1846:74, 95
[100] M'Kerrow, 1846:146, 206
[101] Lorimer, 1842a:93; King, 1846:157; M'Kerrow, 1846:147-178
[102] Lorimer, 1842a:93
[103] Lorimer, 1842a:112
[104] Lorimer, 1842a:139

Church, established in 1847, election by all members in full communion was the practice.[105] This became also the practice in the Free Church of Scotland established in 1843.[106] Lorimer agreed to the ordination of elders, and King would go as far as the laying on of hands, which would be in agreement with the very close relationship he maintained between the ruling and teaching elders and with the practice in the United Secession Church.[107] Of interest is that none of these authors who maintained the divine institution of the ruling elder made any reference to the view of the *Form of Presbyterial Church-Government* which denied the divine institution of this office and considered it only "warrantable."

Twenty years later in 1866, PC Campbell, Principal of the University of Aberdeen, published *The Theory of Ruling Eldership or the position of the lay ruler in the Reformed Churches Examined*. According to him:

He found it regrettable that Calvin supported this theory on "the sole basis" of 1 Tim 5:17. His view was that the acceptance of a valuable institution was hindered by its connection with the presbyter theory.[108] He found sufficient evidence for the office of elder in Rom. 12:8 and especially 1 Cor. 12:28, though he understood the persons referred to in these verses were representatives of the laity designated to take a public and official part in the most important ecclesiastical affairs. Like Dr Samuel Miller of Princeton, who in his essay of 1831 entitled *An Essay on the Warrant, Nature and Duties of the Office of the Ruling Elder*,[109] which Lorimer also admitted had influenced much of his thought in his own work on the eldership of 1841,[110] Campbell appealed to Acts 15:23 and the subsequent history of the church.[111] But according to Campbell, Miller's appeal to these officers in patristic literature as further proof of

---

[105] Rules and Forms UPC, 1883:8
[106] Proceedings FCS, 1843:137. This included the participation of both men and women (Forbes' Digest, 1869:2).
[107] Donald, 1990:45
[108] Campbell, 1866:5
[109] Republished in 1984 as *The Ruling Elder*, by Presbyterian Heritage Publications, Dallas, Texas.
[110] Lorimer, 1842a:xiv
[111] Campbell, 1866:5-8

the "ruling" elder theory, was not correct.[112] They were *seniores plebis*, lay rulers. Campbell believed that the term "elder" referred only to ministers of the Word, and that the theory which claimed lay rulers or councillors in the church to be associated with the presbyter of the Apostolic Church, with appeal to 1 Tim 5:17, must be rejected.[113] This conclusion, he stated, had already been reached by the Westminster Assembly.[114]

By rejecting this theory he did not intend to cause anything negative to the "lay element" (or to the "lay assessors" or "lay assistants," as he preferred to call them) in the church, but he wanted to promote its effectiveness where it existed, "and its extention where it does not."[115] Since it was a lay office, he considered the use of the term "ordination" to designate the formal installation of members of the parochial court inconsistent with the "true view of their position as *seniores plebis* - the representatives of the *unordained* members of the Church."[116] He considered it proper for them to be solemnly set apart for their important duties by prayer.[117] Yet, while promoting the eldership as a popular office, he was hesitant to allow popular election![118] This emphasis on the "lay" character of the eldership was also expressed in the Scottish Church Society.[119] Members of this Society were convinced of the twofold ministry of bishop or presbyter and deacon, as in the Anglican Communion. Principal Story, also choosing for the "lay theory" which saw the status of the elders as representatives of the people, wrote:

The elders were not presbyters in the sense in which the word is identical with *bishops* and *ministers*: they were 'the elders of the people' in the sense in which the term was used in the Old Testament times ... [120]

---

112   Campbell, 1866:8
113   Campbell, 1866:20
114   Campbell, 1866:32
115   Campbell, 1866:4, 63
116   Campbell, 1866:69
117   Campbell, 1866:69
118   Campbell, 1866:71
119   Wright, 1895:270: cf. Sprott, 1882:188 and documents of the Scottish Church Society.
120   Story, 1897:250

A committee of the Pan-Presbyterian Council appointed to enquire into the matter of the office of the elder reported in 1884 that at least three distinct theories were entertained, viz., (1) the New Testament recognises one order of presbyters in which two kinds can be distinguished: teaching and ruling presbyters, (2) there is no warrant in Scripture for the office of elder as it now exists and that elders are not presbyters, and (3) in everything except training and the consequences of training, the elder is the very same as the minister, i.e. overseer, bishop, presbyter and elder.[121] It was found that in practice Presbyterian churches generally followed the first theory. Hill[122] referred to AHK Boyd who stated that "In theory both are presbyters, with no priestly claims. In practice the elders are laymen, the ministers clergymen."

James Cooper, Professor of Ecclesiastical History in Glasgow, in an address to the Church of Scotland Office Bearers' Association of the Presbytery of Dundee in December 1906, was concerned with "a fuller realisation and better discharge of that office of the Eldership."[123] Mindful of the movement toward unity between the Church of Scotland and the United Free Church of Scotland, James Cooper, in agreement with the Westminster divines and PC Campbell, could not find any grounds for the divine institution of a ruling elder. He argued that since the elder was a layman it would be better to refer to him as being "admitted" rather than as being "ordained".[124] Yet, he believed that it was important that the minister be advised and supported by a group of "well-selected lay advisers" in the execution of the authority of the ministerial office.[125] Sir James Balfour, in an address to the Elders' Union in Aberdeen in 1912, rejected the "ruling" elder theory,[126] and Barbour, an elder, in approximately 1935, referred to the "teaching" and "ruling" elder, but did not view the latter as "apostolically authorised."[127]

121	Hill, 1919:251
122	Hill, 1919:251
123	Cooper, 1907:3
124	Cooper, 1907:4
125	Cooper, 1907:5, 8
126	Balfour, 1912:254
127	Barbour, [1935]:1

The Panel on Doctrine had to deal with the offices of the Church of Scotland. Its mandate was mainly to clarify the church's own understanding of various aspects of its ministry in light of the issue of women in the eldership and ministry of the church, as well as in light of ecumenical exposure. The first report to be completed and adopted by the General Assembly in 1963 was *A Brief Statement on the Office of the Elder in the Church of Scotland*. This report stated that the eldership was a spiritual office concerned with the rule and pastoral oversight of a congregation.[128] An attempt to introduce the "lay" theory of the elder was rejected by the presbyteries. The description of the eldership as a "spiritual office, held by laymen" which had been in the draft sent down to the presbyteries the previous year, was omitted from the final Statement.[129] The office of elder was considered to be distinct from, yet closely associated with the ministry of Word and sacraments, and at that stage restricted to men only.[130] Admission to the office was to be by prayer after the preaching of the Word, the answering of a prescribed question and the signing of a formulary similar to that signed by ministers. This was considered to be the ordination of an elder, though there was no laying on of hands. The difference in the ordination of the ministers and elders was explained as due to the difference in their responsibilities and functions. The elder's ordination was for life.[131] His duties were described as both corporate and individual. The corporate duties referred to functions and responsibilities in the church session, which included planning of and assisting in holy communion, and seeing to it that all children of members were baptised. Maintenance of church records, admission of members to the church and holy communion, exercise of discipline, supervision of congregational activities, instruction of members and control of congregational properties were all part of the elder's corporate duties.[132] Individual duties referred to responsibilities in the elder's district and the elder's personal behaviour. In addition the

---

[128] Report, 1963:757
[129] Report, 1962:823
[130] Report, 1963:757
[131] Report, 1963:757
[132] Report, 1963:758

elder had responsibilities in the other courts of the church when elected thereto.[133]

As requested by the General Assembly of 1963, the Panel on Doctrine presented a report on the Scriptural basis of the eldership to the Assembly of 1964[134]. In giving an historical overview of the office of the elder since the reformation, the panel emphasised that this office was more in line with the deacon of the early church.[135] On New Testament evidence for the eldership as it was known in the Church of Scotland, the panel made an appeal to scholarship that "overwhelming" had been forced to the conclusion that there is no evidence for today's elder in Scripture.[136] The explanation given by the panel as to why this elder was in the church was that it resulted from some sort of confusion at the time of the reformation of the Church of Scotland, since even Calvin obviously did not know this elder. What should have been called "deacon" was called "elder."[137] Tracing the roots of the present day elder back to the "diakonein" of the New Testament, the report concluded that the office which had developed out of this service established at the time of Acts 6:1-6 was not related to alms, poor relief, and the ingathering of funds for these purposes, but to a ministry of deaconing discharged by the apostles through the Word, complemented by that of the Seven - a situation that was not reproduced later.[138] During the period of 1 Tim 3:1-13 a distinct office became evident in the life of the church. What happened was that "deaconing had 'bifurcated' into overseer (Bishop) and Servant (Deacon)."[139] The panel concluded that there was no clear evidence in the Bible for the title "elder" as it is known today, but it is war-

---

[133] Report, 1963:759. To the same Assembly was handed in a report by the same committee on the office of the minister, titled *Statement on the Christian Ministry*. The fact of two separate reports and their difference in title seems to confirm these offices as two different "positions" in the church. The one a "ministry" the other not, but a position.
[134] Report, 1964:751
[135] Report, 1964:755
[136] Report, 1964:756
[137] Report, 1964:756
[138] Report, 1964:757
[139] Report, 1963:757

ranted: "There is evidence in the New Testament of officials of the Church who did just what our Elders do to-day. These were the Deacons."[140]

This second attempt at importing an official statement on the two-fold ministry, that of presbyter and deacon, into the Church of Scotland, did not succeed. After consideration of the responses by presbyteries and other individuals to this statement, a revised statement on the Scriptural basis of the eldership was presented to the General Assembly of 1967. The Panel on Doctrine, on the basis of Scripture (with reference to concepts like diaconia, presbuteros, episcopos, leitourgos, proistamenos, and diakonos) and the Form of Presbyterial Church-Government, concluded that the New Testament gives no picture of the office of the elder as it is known today.[141] It was not prescribed in the New Testament, but it was entirely in accord with the nature of the ministries which were to be found there.[142]

In this report, received by the General Assembly who did not express approval of it,[143] the view on "diakonia" is more clearly defined.[144] It stated that the ministry of the Lord is the pattern for all ministry; the ministry of the people of God follows the pattern of that of Christ. Within this total ministry of the people of God there are special ministries by and through which the total ministry is guided and sustained.[145] It explained that as early as Acts 6 there was a division of the ministry into the "Ministry (diakonia) of the Word, and prayer (which remained an apostolic function), and the 'serving of the Tables' which is a response to the Word."[146] By the end of the first century "the Serving of the Tables", or "Ministry of Response to the Word," took on the greater definition of a specific office and was undertaken by those who acted as the representatives of the people of God to lead and prompt them to undertake that ministry which belonged to them, and to share with the minister in the government and oversight of the church. The panel considered this office to be far more significant and richer than the

---

140	Report, 1964:757
141	Report, 1967:230-231
142	Report, 1967:231
143	Report, 1967:236
144	Report, 1967:230
145	Report, 1967:232
146	Report, 1967:232

church had made it to appear. They considered it capable of including a wide variety of functions, depending upon the gifts of the individuals who were appointed to the office. It could include both men and women.[147] The panel's viewpoint was that the eldership arose from this ministry. The elders acted as representatives of the people and performed the "Ministry (diakonia) of Reponse to the Word". Their primary task was to "seek the fruit of the Word sown amongst the people" as they assisted the minister to exercise rule over the flock.[148] The panel concluded that in the Church of Scotland from its earlier days there had been a solemn public admission of elders to office by prayer and the taking of vows or oaths of faithfulness. The word ordination was used for this admission. Ordination in this context was defined by the nature of the office for which those elected were set apart.[149]

The Panel on Doctrine would again, at a later time, attempt to convince the Church of Scotland to accept this theory on the origin, status and position of the elder. In this the panel enjoyed the support of TF Torrance. In line with PC Campbell (1866), he appealed to the Westminster Assembly to reject the association of the office of elder with the "presbyter" of the New Testament. Torrance related it to the diaconate of the church. He considered the Scottish elder to be more like the "deacon" of the Pastoral Epistles.[150] It was essentially a "sacramental office"[151] belonging to the *kleros*[152] even though they "do not belong to the priesthood as such."[153] He was convinced that an eldership patterned after the biblical and early Christian diaconate would recover something of its wholeness as an essential spiritual and evangelical *diaconia*.[154] He ignored any "governing function" that the elder might have had.

---

[147] Report, 1967:232
[148] Report, 1967:233
[149] Report, 1967:233
[150] Torrance, 1984:509
[151] Torrance, 1984:513
[152] Torrance, 1984:514
[153] Torrance, 1984:514
[154] Torrance, 1984:518

5.4 The presbyter and Scottish Presbyterianism

That no theology of the ministry of the offices developed in Scottish reformed church polity is reflected in the diversity of opinion on the place and function of the various offices.

The priority of the office of the minister was upheld in the Scottish church. This office was considered as a highest position in a clerical sense. The other offices were co-workers or assistants and not considered in terms of ministries distinct from that of the minister. Further twentieth century consideration of the office of the minister would attempt to emphasise it as the actual presbyter.

From the development of the office of the elder in the course of history and the inconclusive views on its place and function in the Scottish church, it is clear that the office of the elder did not develop as a ministry in its own right. The reason for this is that this office was considered an assistant to the minister along episcopal lines. The major cause for this development is the conviction that what can be done by the lower office can be done by the higher, because the higher possesses the power of the lower. The consequences of the compromise between the reformed conception of the offices with episcopacy is reflected in this development.

The diversity of opinion on the place and function of the Scottish reformed elder within the context of the ministry of the church was continued in reflections on its place and function in the church during the latter part of the twentieth century.

CHAPTER 6

THE DEACON

It was especially the office of the deacon that was neglected in Scottish Presbyterianism and denied its rightful place as a ministry in the church.

6.1 An overview

During the latter half of the seventeenth century, deacons were not commonly found. As early as 1652, James Guthrie, in his *A Treatise of Ruling Elders and Deacons*, besides considering the office of deacon as of "the lowest rank,"[1] mentioned as a defect and fault in some congregations

> that they put no difference betwixt these two but so confound and mingle them together, as if they were both one, either appointing none for the office of Deacon, but leaving that charge also upon elders, or else giving the Deacons the same power and employment with the elders.[2]

Foster[3] was of the opinion that during the Restoration period, 1661-1688, deacons were scarce but not unheard of. He drew attention to an interesting occurance during the Restoration period - the ordination of a deacon by the Bishop of Orkney in 1683.

> [The oath being tendered] with all the ceremonial usual in such cases, [the Bishop] gave him full power to administer the Sacrament of Baptisme, and to give the benefits of marriage, to visit the sick, keep sessions, or any other office that are incumbent

---

[1] Lorimer, 1842a:34
[2] Lorimer, 1842a:51
[3] Foster, 1958:98

for a deacon to performe, restricting him only from the actual consecration of the Lord's Supper.[4]

A 1705 overture presented to the General Assembly reminded that "in parochial sessions deacons were admitted with respect to their special care and oversight of the poor of the parish."[5] Walter Steuart of Pardovan in 1709, depicting early eighteenth century practice, repeated Guthrie's complaint. According to him, the office of the deacon was of divine institution; "it is an unwarrantable omission in some congregations, that either they put no difference betwixt elders and deacons, or else they neglect to appoint any to the office of deacon."[6] The thought apparently prevailing during his time was that the elder was a deacon. This, however, could not allow him to accept the absence of deacons: "Albeit the pastor includes the office of doctor, elder and deacon, yet seeing these are of divine institution" implied that nothing may be added, but it also meant, according to Steuart, "nothing ought to be diminished therefrom."[7]

In 1719 the deacon received the attention of the General Assembly. It was recommended to all ministers to take care that deacons as well as elders be ordained in such congregations where deacons were wanting.[8] In a rather careless statement by Dickson[9] it was implied that the demise of the office of the deacon during the eighteenth century should be laid before the door of the Moderates of that century. He accused Moderatism of having done its best to

> degrade the office (of the eldership) by confounding its functions with those of the deaconship; - distributing the communion elements, and standing at the plate at the church door being considered as much as could reasonably be expected of men who had solemnly undertaken a spiritual office![10]

---

[4] Foster, 1958:98. This reflects the influence of the English Church on the restored Episcopal Church of Scotland during the period of the Restoration.
[5] Henderson, 1934:60
[6] Compendium, Part 1:210
[7] Compendium, Part 1:211
[8] AGA 1638-1842:529
[9] Dickson, 1871:4
[10] Dickson, 1871:4

The fact was that despite efforts by Thomas Chalmers, at the beginning of the nineteenth century, to revive this office in Glasgow,[11] and despite Lorimer's disagreement that the office of deacon was neglected,[12] the office was not retained.

According to Lorimer deacons were not scarce. He held that:

> From the above period (1719) down, comparatively speaking, to the modern days, the office of the deacon, as a distinct office in the Church of Scotland, has to a great extend been in abeyance, and that its leading duties in the case of the poor have been neglected; far from it. They have been excellently discharged - only blended with those of the elders.[13]

He had already in his *The Eldership of the Church of Scotland*, which was first printed in 1841, pointed out that in his time deacons were "conjoined" with elders.[14] This was in contrast with the Dutch Church. Lorimer referred to Dr Stevens who set down his observations of Dutch practice in *A Brief view of the Dutch Ecclesiastical Establishment* written in 1838. Stevens wrote that the office of the deacon was in vigorous operation in the Dutch Church. Those who held this office in larger towns had a court of meeting of their own, "and so important is the office deemed that in conjunction with the elders, the deacons have the appointment of the ministry."[15]

GW Sprott, in a sermon preached before the Synod of Lothian in 1877, complained that for the most part the "Diaconate," "which our Standards declare to be an Apostolic ministry, designed to watch over the sacred secularities of the Church," had been given up.[16] At the same time Sprott put into words what might have been the thought of many,

---

[11] In his efforts to fight pauperism he introduced a large staff of elders and deacons, each of whom was to superintend a proportion or district of the parish, and to acquaint himself with every inhabitant. He held that the duties of the office of the deacon and that of the elder could not be completely fulfilled by one man (Drummond and Bullock, 1973:173); Brown, 1982:132ff

[12] Henderson, 1934:72; Drummond and Bullock, 1973:173

[13] Lorimer, 1842b:94

[14] Lorimer, 1842a:86

[15] Lorimer, 1842b:50

[16] Sprott, 1877:9

and gave a new function to this office "which our most eminent writers have regarded as the divinely appointed nursery for the Presbyterate."[17] In 1882 he wrote that this office is "almost extinct."[18] His fellow member in the Scottish Church Society, the Rev. Thomas Leishman, wrote in 1895 that this office survived in a "state of suspended animation."[19]

A revival of the office was experienced in the Free Church established after the 1843 Disruption. In the statistical accounts of the 1929 united Church of Scotland the office of the deacon is, however, no longer indicated as a distinct office in this church.[20]

6.2 The place and duty of the deacon

A characteristic of the history of the Scottish deacon was that, in practice, its position and functions remained unclear. The *Second Book of Discipline* and the Westminster *Form of Presbyterial Church-Government* were against the inclusion of deacons in the kirk session, yet their presence was considered by some to be convenient. In 1659 a difference of opinion on the matter of voting arose in Aberdeen when some maintained that deacons had no vote at all in the sessions and therefore none in election. Others declared that the Act of 1649 left the voting not to the elders but to the members of the session, and that it was well known that deacons as well as the elders were members of the session.[21] According to Steuart of Pardovan, the duties of the deacon were mainly confined to financial matters. But deacons were also considered to "provide the elements, to carry them, and serve the communicants at the Lord's table,[22] and they attended session

---

[17] Sprott, 1877:9; It is somewhat difficult to know exactly what Sprott meant by this - a nursery for "lay" elders, or a nursery for the ministry of Word and sacraments as in the case of episcopal practice - since he maintained a twofold ministry of bishop or presbyter and the deacon (Sprott, 1882:188). Steuart of Pardovan also considered the diaconate as a nursery, but more clearly, for the eldership (Compendium, Part 1:268).

[18] Sprott, 1882:220

[19] Leishman, 1895:51

[20] Reports, 1931-1990

[21] Henderson, 1935:69

[22] Compendium, Part 1:212

meetings", "not for discipline, but for what relates to their own office."[23] Deacons, the General Assembly of 1719 stated: "shall have no decisive voice in calling of ministers, or in the exercise of Church discipline."[24] Lorimer was convinced that "Few pretences could be more absurd than that the deaconship involved more than the care of secular interests."[25]

David King gave an altogether new interpretation to the "serving of the tables." He was convinced that the "serving of the tables, or in other words, the management of ecclesiastical funds, was the proper and special task of the deacons."[26] However, he would have preferred that the church he belonged to - the United Presbyterian Church - set apart the managers to their functions by regular and solemn ordination.[27] John M'Kerrow was convinced that the deacon had no spiritual function but that his proper function was the management of ecclesiastical funds. He rejected any appeal to Acts 6 as "having no reference whatever either to providing or distributing the sacramental elements at the table of the Lord."[28] Since deacons were mere "helps" or assistants to the elders he rejected the idea of a separate deacon's court.[29]

With the revival of the office of the deacon in the Free Church of Scotland, a Deacons' Court was introduced for the purpose of managing the secular affairs of the church.[30] The duties of the office-bearers of this Court included paying special attention to the secular affairs of the congregation, attending to the gathering of the people's contributions for the support of the ministry and receiving donations for other ecclesiastical purposes, attending to the poor of the congregation, and

---

[23] Compendium, Part 1:216
[24] AGA 1638-1842:529; Compendium, Part 1:180
[25] Lorimer, 1842b:34
[26] King, 1844:88. M'Kerrow held the same view (M'Kerrow, 1846:249).
[27] King, 1844:89
[28] M'Kerrow, 1846:199; Struthers, historian of the Relief Church, pointed out that the ordinary office of this Church included the deacon where necessary for serving the table and conducting the secular affairs of the Church (Struthers, 1843:439).
[29] M'Kerrow, 1846:250-252
[30] Forbes' Digest, 1869:4

watching over the education of the children of the poor.[31] Along with the elders the deacons could receive the Sabbath collection and were expected to visit their districts.[32] The provision was made that where there were not enough deacons, elders could be employed as deacons.[33] Deacons were also permitted to assist the elders with advice in the church sessions, and provide and carry the elements. However, it was considered more appropriate that the latter, together with serving at the Lord's table, was done by the elders.[34] The membership of the Deacon's Court included the minister and elders as well. The argument was "that according to the theory of the Presbyterian Church, the greater office includes the less; the ministers and elders are therefore deacons, and as such, sit and act as members of this court."[35] The office of the deacon was considered to be "one of relief or assistance to the Pastor and Ruling Elders, with a view to their greater freedom in the prosecution of their higher functions, ... "[36] After election the deacons were ordained and their office was for life, though resignations could be accepted.[37] A Free Church writer, John Macpherson, at the end of the nineteenth century, agreed that a person could not be a deacon unless ordained.[38] He further emphasised that the office of the deacon was indeed a "permanent ecclesiastical office" but that it could not be regarded as a "spiritual function."[39]

In the United Secession (1733) and Relief (1761) Churches, which formed the United Presbyterian Church in 1847, the office of deacon was recognised but it viewed as manager of ecclesiastical affairs. The general practice was to have a body of managers who were not

---

[31] It must be kept in mind that with the Free Church of Scotland now standing outside establishment, maintenance of the ministry was solely in the hands of the church itself. In this regard the task of maintenance of the ministry was now added to the financial responsibilities of the deacon. This could also, to a great extend, explain the revival of this office in this church.
[32] Forbes' Digest, 1869:4-5
[33] Forbes' Digest, 1869:5
[34] Forbes' Digest, 1869:5
[35] Forbes' Digest, 1869:5
[36] Practice FCS, 1886:23
[37] Forbes' Digest, 1869:6
[38] Macpherson, [1883]:99
[39] Macpherson, [1883]:95

ordained, but who were responsible for congregational finance. This remained the practice despite overtures which were sent to the United Presbyterian Church Synod the next year desiring the restoration of the Deacon to its rightful place.[40] Later still the *Rules and Forms of Procedures* of this church stated that "it is the duty of the session to see that the poor of the congregation have suitable aid in their necessities." It also said that where there were no deacons the poor fund was to be administered by the session.[41]

As late as 1888, the Church of Scotland called for a precise definition of the relationship of deacons to elders. The General Assembly agreed that deacons could sit with elders only when specifically called to discuss finances but that they had no vote even concerning such issues.[42] In this respect church appointments could be for a short time. This short term diaconate, which was nothing more than a board of management, was open to women.

Matters did not improve for the deacon during the twentieth century. After the union of the United Free Church of Scotland and the Church of Scotland in 1929, there was no uniform arrangement for dealing with finances and charity: the former systems existed side by side. The method that became the practice was that of the Congregational Board which included ministers and elders, and a corresponding number of members from the congregation, both men and women.[43] At the same time the United Church also acknowledged a Deacon's Court,[44] which had been the practice of the old United Free Church of Scotland and appeared to be a different name for the Congregational Board. In the case of the Deacon's Court, men were ordained for life.

In reply to a petition presented to the General Assembly meeting in 1931 to break down the barriers that prevented the ordination of women to the ministry, the eldership and the diaconate, it was reported in 1932 that the diaconate as understood and practised in the Church of Scotland

---

[40] Proceedings UPC, 1848:170-172
[41] Henderson, 1935:73; Rules and Forms UPC, 1895:7, 62
[42] Henderson, 1935:70; 1954:84
[43] Cox, 1934:119; Henderson, 1954:86
[44] Cox, 1934:120

dealt mainly with the financial affairs of the congregation.[45] The committee reported that the diaconate was far removed from the general operation in the church, "nor is it in any way essential to the completeness of the Presbyterian system."[46] Although satisfaction could not be given to admit women to the ministry of the Word and sacraments, and the eldership, the General Assembly of 1935, with the consent of the majority of the presbyteries, enacted that the life diaconate may be held by women.[47]

GD Henderson maintained that "no one had any doubt that the deacon in the Reformed Church was a kind of assistant elder, certainly inferior in rank, and that whatever a deacon do was a proper function of an elder. The 'greater includes the less'."[48] In 1955, JKS Reid complained that a diaconate that concerned itself with the material and financial interests of a congregation did not have much resemblance to the deaconing of the tables as instituted in the New Testament.[49] And, in 1966, he wrote that the inclusion of the diaconate within the spiritual government of the church did not mean that it enjoyed equality with other offices. To support his opinion he appealed to Calvin. The concept of rank had to be taken into account. He stated that "Deacons rank after both pastors and governors."[50]

The confusion surrounding the office of deacon was aptly illustrated by GD Henderson. In his work of 1935, *The Scottish Ruling Elder*, the chapter on the "Elder at the Plate" dealt with a history of the office of the deacon. The author concluded the chapter with these words: "The elder [sic] is at the plate in view of his responsibility as collector and distributor of money ... ."[51]

A different approach to the deacon presented itself in the work of the Scoto-Catholics. By the end of the second decade of the twentieth century, Wotherspoon and Kirkpatrick published their *A Manual of Church Doctrine*. Contrary to the *Second Book of Discipline*'s distinction

---

[45] Report, 1933:1174
[46] Report, 1993:1174
[47] Report, 1935:xxvi
[48] Henderson, 1934:61
[49] Reid, 1955:30-31
[50] Reid, 1966;101
[51] Henderson, 1935:98

of a threefold "sort of office-beiraris,"[52] and basing their arguments on the *Westminster Form of Presbyterial Government*, they emphasised a two-fold order of ministry: the presbyter or bishop and the deacon.[53] The deacons were to be the assistants to the presbyters.[54] Differing from Anglican practice, they considered the functions of the deacon to be restricted to "distributing the necessity of the poor,"[55] and they complained that the position of the diaconate was "anomalous and unsatisfactory," much of their functions being absorbed by the "lay Eldership."[56] In their view, what was being done by the "lay elder" should have been in the hands of the deacon. This complaint was repeated by TF Torrance and RS Wright publishing a revised version of this book in 1960.[57] According to them

> it seems very clear that the Scottish Elder more nearly reproduces the deacon or deacon-elder of the Early Church than the 'deacon' in any of the other churches today. His office was essentially diaconal and complementary to that of the Presbyter who is ordained to dispense the Word and Sacraments.[58]

In the defining of the two-fold order in this manner they were preceded by Sprott. According to Sprott, there were only two orders in the ministry: the bishop or presbyter and the deacon.[59] The movement to this two-fold order of ministry seemed to be found amongst those sympathetic to Anglican episcopalianism.

The office of deacon failed to be representative of the ministry of diaconia in the Church of Scotland. Restricting the diaconate to the care of the poor and the management of ecclesiastical material affairs led to the eventual "fading" away of the office of the deacon. Having lost its duties to the elder, there appeared to be no further need for this office.

---

[52] Compendium, Part 1:112
[53] Wotherspoon and Kirkpatrick, [1920]:152, 157
[54] Wotherspoon and Kirkpatrick, [1920]:152
[55] Wotherspoon and Kirkpatrick, [1920]:175
[56] Wotherspoon and Kirkpatrick, [1920]:175
[57] Wotherspoon and Kirkpatrick, 1960:100
[58] Wotherspoon and Kirkpatrick, 1960:100
[59] Sprott, 1882:188

The diaconate, however, was an important ministry of the church. If it could not express itself through the traditional office of the deacon, it did so in other ways.

6.3 The revival of the diaconate

In 1887 an "Order of Deaconesses" was established in the Church of Scotland,[60] but it did not have any reference to the office of deacon. Dr AH Charteris, who visited the original Mother-House in Kaiserswerth, Germany, was the chief instigator of the introduction of this Order.[61] He appealed to Scripture for the revival of this Order, but it appears that the Order followed a pragmatic development in the Church of Scotland.[62] The committee reporting to the General Assembly of 1956 was not convinced that Charteris intended an *office* of deaconesses.[63] As the deaconesses had not been given any specific ecclesiastical status in the Church of Scotland, a Scheme of 1949 sought to enhance their status by providing that they should be commissioned by a presbytery and those who qualified given the right to preach.[64] The Scheme proposed in 1955 continued these two provisions.[65] The Special Committee anent the Order of Deaconesses of the General Assembly of the Church of Scotland did not, however, accept a thesis presented by the deaconesses which stated:

> The word 'deaconess' both in the New Testament and in the history of the church refers to an office in the church. Hence, the 'order' of deaconesses must refer to an order of ministry in the church, and not to any voluntary association, group or sisterhood of Christian Women.[66]

The committee did not deal with this issue, for two reasons. One was due to "a lack of time," and the other was because the committee was

---

[60] Report, 1956:793; This followed the appointment of a Committee by the Alliance of Presbyterian Churches which met in Belfast in 1880 to consider the propriety of reviving the Scripture order of Deaconesses (Charteris, 1905;147).
[61] Report, 1956:794
[62] Report, 1956:794
[63] Report, 1956:794
[64] Report, 1956:795
[65] Report, 1956:795
[66] Report, 1956:792

CHAPTER 6 141

convinced that this issue would demand much research and discussion, besides the fact that it implied a change to the constitution of the church.[67] The committee's proposal was that the matter be referred to a more permanent body to take up the fundamental issues involved in the thesis.[68] As a result, the issue was remitted to a Committee on the Order of Deaconesses instituted in 1956.[69] The committee was instructed by the Assembly to "make use of such expert consultation as may be necessary and of material made available by the World Council of Churches and the World Presbyterian Alliance."[70] An interim report was presented to the General Assembly in 1957 and again in 1958. The committee reported that it was sufficient to note that a Diaconate of Women was agreeable to the Word of God.[71] Though the diaconate of women disappeared from the Western Church after the Council of Nimes in 394, the committee appreciated its revival in the Church of Scotland. New in the report was that the concept 'to deacon' was brought into relation with the human service and sacrifice of Christ on the cross.[72] The committee proceeded very carefully stating that

> it is not possible, however, to draw but inspiration from the use of the word 'to deacon' in the New Testament. It cannot be established that in any place it is used to describe the official function of the Diaconate."[73]

Nevertheless, an important though tentative development seemed to have begun in the thinking of the Church of Scotland with regard to the diaconate in the church.

The same committee stressed the modification of some of the assumptions in the Scheme for the Order of Deaconesses accepted in 1956. For one thing, it said that the *office* of the deaconess should now

---

[67] Report, 1956:793
[68] Report, 1956:793
[69] Report, 1958:655
[70] Report, 1978:653
[71] Report, 1958:655
[72] Report, 1958:655
[73] Report, 1958:655; The use of the word 'diaconate" in the context of this Committee's report, as well as previous Committees on this issue, appears to have been restricted to reference to the work of the deaconness only.

be emphasised, rather than the *order* of deaconesses.[74] The matter was referred to the newly established Committee anent the place of Women in the Church.

This committee reported to the Assembly of 1960 that "if they are to be received in their own right as Deaconesses, the Church will need to face up to an even more radical change in its polity than that of admitting women to the Eldership."[75] The committee observed that in historical fact the diaconate, as the counterpart of the apostolic ministry, differed from it in that it included both men and women.[76] Furthermore, there seemed reason to believe that women, though they may not have been formally appointed, held the recognised office of Deaconess in the early church as an *office* in the ministry.[77] The conclusion was that the revival of the office of Deaconess in the Church of Scotland was the revival of a Scriptural office and there seemed to be no Scriptural reason against "the conception of a Kirk Session being composed of Minister, Elders (men and women), and Deaconesses, the Deaconess sitting in her own right as holding an office in the Ministry."[78] At the request of the Committee on the Order of Deaconesses, the Panel on Doctrine, which was established as a committee of the General Assembly in 1960, dealt with the meaning of the word *office* in their report to the Assembly of 1962.[79] They found that the word had several meanings in the life of the church, and that there was no objection to its use in the Scheme of Order of Deaconesses. The panel did not find that there were any clear and indisputable references to the office of deaconess in the Holy Scripture, but it did believe the deaconess to be not inconsistent therewith.[80] The actual acknowledgment of the deaconess as an office in the church was avoided. In 1989, however, in the report of the Panel on Doctrine, the membership to the diaconate was described as:

> The members of the diaconate are full-time salaried servants of the Church, who have received residential training and are

---

[74] Report, 1958:958
[75] Report, 1960:823
[76] Report, 1960:823
[77] Report, 1960:823
[78] Report, 1960:823
[79] Report, 1962:821
[80] Report, 1962:821

equiped to supplement the leadership of the congregation in which they serve.[81]

It was explained that there were two kinds of diaconal workers within the Church of Scotland: the deaconess whose task it was to organise and mobilise the women of the congregation and who received no salary, and the parish sisters first employed in 1906, who visited the sick and the elderly. The union of 1929 brought together the sisters of the United Free Church of Scotland with the parish sisters of the Church of Scotland and training was established at St. Column's College. In 1950 all came together within a single Order of Deaconesses. The report continued that when the eldership and the ministry was opened for women as well as men it was realised that the deaconess did not simply exercise "women's" ministry but carried out a complementary form of service. In 1979 the diaconate was opened to both men and women.[82] The men were called deacons.

This diaconate was now described as a distinct office "complementary to that of the Ministry of the Word and Sacraments."[83] By 1989, the main duties of these deacons and deaconesses included fulltime engagement in services of an evangelistic, educational, or social nature within a parish or within an institution or sphere of activity recognised by the General Assembly. They also had permission to preach.[84] They were considered to be part of a team with the minister and the elders of a congregation. The Panel of Doctrine, therefore, found it necessary to recommend to the General Assembly of 1989 that the members of the diaconate should have a recognised place in the courts of the Church.[85]

This was an important development, but without any reference to the traditional office of the deacon in the Church of Scotland. Of importance, however, was the increased emphasis on the diaconate as "a complementary service to the Ministry of Word and Sacraments." On the one hand this represented a major shift away from traditional Scottish ecclesiological consideration of the offices in terms of positions with

---

[81] Report, 1989:203
[82] Report, 1989:203
[83] Report, 1989:203
[84] Report, 1989:203
[85] Report, 1989:204

constituted functions and from the understanding of the deacon as a mere assistant. On the other hand a development in the direction of a liturgical office seemed possible.

This shift in emphasis from "position" to "service" formed part of a wider rethinking of the ministry of the Church of Scotland and reflected participation in ecumenical debates. However, it met with opposition because it neglected to take into account traditional convictions and practice.

Despite a revival of the office of the deacon in the mid-nineteenth century Free Church of Scotland, the office of the deacon did not develop into a complete and independent ministry within Scottish presbyterianism as was the case in the French and Dutch Reformed traditions. This was because of the compromise between reformed presbyterial ecclesiology with an episcopal conception of the church and its offices. In episcopalianism the office of the deacon as assistant to the bishop holds an important position and function in liturgy and administration. In addition, it is the first step to the priesthood. In Scottish presbyterianism the understanding of the offices in terms of rank and dignity was taken over from episcopacy. The deacon developed as an assistant to the elder. The conviction, however, that the higher office includes the lower led to the fusion of the functions of the deacon with that of the elder. This prevented the development of the office of the deacon as a ministry in its own right.

The fact that the office of the deacon did not develop as an independent ministry within Scottish presbyterianism left a void within the ministry of the Scottish presbyterian church. This is reflected in the reinstatement of the order of the deaconess. In the development of this order, eventually understood to be an office in the church which included men as well, no return was made to a reflection on the reformed office of the deacon. In its later development the Scottish presbyterian diaconate represented a return to the episcopal deacon. The reason for this is found in the fact that in Scottish presbyterianism the offices were not considered, in accordance with the presbyterial-synodical approach to church government with its starting point the offices, as service to the ministry of Christ, but they are considered as positions in an institution.

CHAPTER 7

TWENTIETH CENTURY ECUMENICAL CONVERSATIONS AND SCOTTISH PRESBYTERIAN OFFICES

AS IN THE CASE OF NINETEENTH AND EARLY TWENTIETH CENTURY RECONstruction of Scottish presbyterianism the concern of the twentieth century ecumenical movement was more and more toward organic unity between churches. A major difficulty was reconciling the offices of the different traditions. This was discussed in conversations on church unity between the Church of Scotland and the Anglican Communion. At the same time the Church of Scotland concerned itself with a reconsideration of its offices in the light of its own needs. Different viewpoints on the place and function of the offices and their inter-relatedness in the church were presented along two major lines - those inclined to an episcopal approach to the government of the church and those in favour of government by presbyters in assembly. The wide range of opinions on the offices reflects the consequences of the continued consideration of the offices as positions in the church as an institution and underlines the incomplete development in Scottish reformed ecclesiology in the area of the ministry of the offices in the church.

In these discussions the sixteenth and seventeenth century emphasis on Scripture and confession in determining the viewpoint of the church was replaced by an emphasis on traditional historical associations.

7.1 Ecumenical conversations and the offices of the church

In church union discussions with the Anglican Communion, a major concern of the presbyterian participants was to reconcile presbyterian and episcopalian ministerial orders. A crucial issue was the validity of the presbyterian ordained ministry. As early as 1933 the Church of Scotland instructed her members participating in the first series of church union conversations with the Anglican Communion that

> any agreement with regard to Order and Sacraments of the conferring Churches must be based on the recognition of the equal validity of the Order and Sacraments of the conferring Churches, and the equal standing of the accepted communicants and ordained ministry of each.[1]

The validity of the presbyterian ordained ministry was one of the major concerns of the members of the Scottish Church Society who were seeking a solution along Anglican lines.

GW Sprott, who was one of the leading figures in this Society and author of the standard work, *The Worship and Offices of the Church of Scotland* (1882), was convinced that all reformed churches held that there were only two orders in the ministry of divine appointment: the bishop or presbyter and the deacon, with prelates belonging to the same order as presbyters.[2] The preaching presbyters were the successors of the apostles in all the ordinary functions of the official ministry.[3] Sprott believed that a "rightly constituted ministry"[4] with "definite arrangements for its perpetuity"[5] was essential to the proper existence of the church. To participate in this ministry, a person must have been appointed thereto by a lawful ordination by those who had the power to ordain.[6] He maintained that there was no hope for Christian reunion except on the basis of a ministry derived by succession from apostolic times.[7] Wotherspoon, in a Scottish Church Society publication discussing Scottish ministerial reunion with reference to the Church of Scotland and the Scottish Episcopal Church, stated that the presbyterate was the fundamental order and contained the power of transmission.[8]

The point at issue for these authors was that there was no real difference between the ministerial succession in the episcopal church and that

---

[1] Report, 1933:1016
[2] Sprott, 1882:188
[3] Sprott, 1882:187-188
[4] Sprott, 1877:9
[5] Sprott, 1873:13
[6] Sprott, 1882:187; 1873:8, 17
[7] Sprott, 1882:202
[8] Wotherspoon, 1909:19

in the presbyterian church. Within the context of reunion debates, Sprott's viewpoint was that the Anglicans must admit that the Church of Scotland had an unbroken ministerial succession from the ancient Scottish church.[9] Leishman stated that

> to the historic eye Episcopacy is but a phase of Presbytery, and Presbytery a form of Episcopacy in which the necessary office of oversight is held in common by a college of Presbyters.[10]

The basis of Anglican Unity was laid down by the Lambeth Conference of 1888. This basis was not the Thirty-nine Articles, but what came to be known as the "Lambeth Quadrilateral" of Bible, creeds, sacraments, and historic episcopate. The possession of an episcopate in historical succession from the Apostles was put forward as an essential condition for full intercommunion with the Church of England.[11]

GMS Walker, writing during the 1950s in connection with reunion discussions between the Church of Scotland and the Church of England, attempted a synthesis of episcopacy and presbytery. He complained that presbyterianism tended to be "a misleading name. It suggests the absence of any office superior to that which in Anglican and Roman terminology is called the priesthood."[12] The minister must be called, "not a parish priest, but a parish bishop."[13] He argued that from studying the Bible, the Scriptural solution appeared obvious to the Scottish reformers: "continue the episcopal ministry of Word and Sacraments and discipline, but put the parish in place of the diocese as the unit of administration."[14] The ancient three-fold order of bishop, presbyter and deacon could be retained on the level of the parish; but above that level, the application of conciliar doctrine replaced a hierarchy of persons with a hierarchy of courts, and at the summit there was the General Assembly, "with popular mandate, in open debate, by free speech, as an ecclesiastical Parliament, would guarantee the freedom of the Church."[15] The minister,

---

[9] Sprott, 1895:64; This was also the conviction of Wotherspoon.
[10] Leishman, 1909:53
[11] Bronkhorst, 1947:251
[12] Walker, 1955:238
[13] Walker, 1955:238
[14] Walker, 1955:243
[15] Walker, 1955:243-244

according to him, was always distinguished from the elder and occupied the place "not of a Presbyter, but of a bishop; in practice he has constantly claimed and exercised those precise powers which are episcopal."[16] And, the presbytery, "in dignity," resembled "rather the Convocation of a Province, for it is a conclave of Presbyters and Bishops."[17] Walker stated that he could find no historical reason why Anglicans denied "Presbyterian orders," or debarred presbyterians from communion.[18]

In a report presented to the General Assembly of 1957 an attempt was made to remain faithful to the Anglican position. This was done despite the insistence of the General Assembly of 1934, in response to the *Joint Report* and the *Joint Statement of Agreements* on Anglican and Presbyterian Conversations presented to the General Assembly of that year, that mutual recognition of the ministry and communicants was necessary in discussions on church union.[19] Conversations between the Church of Scotland and the Church of England started in 1932 but faded out by 1939. They were resumed in 1949 resulting in the report *Relations between Anglican and Presbyterian Churches. Being a Joint Report presented by the Representatives of the Church of England, the Church of Scotland, the Episcopal Church in Scotland, and the Presbyterian Church of England: January 1957* which was presented to the General Assembly meeting of 1957.

The so-called "Bishop's Report"[20] of 1957 concentrated on finding a policy acceptable to both churches and on pointing out agreements between the presbyterian and episcopal polities.[21] To facilitate union between the two Churches it was urged that the General Assembly institute bishops in the Church of Scotland as a prelude to union.[22] The reason given was that from the Anglican side it was clear that intercommunion was not possible apart from episcopacy.[23] The writers

---

[16] Walker, 1955:247
[17] Walker, 1955:249-250
[18] Walker, 1955:254
[19] Report, 1934:1016
[20] Brown, 1987:239
[21] Report, 1957:76-99
[22] Report, 1957:86ff
[23] Report, 1957:83, 86

of the Report found a common denominator in the concept *episcopé*. The two systems of church government, episcopalianism and presbyterianism, were considered to be basically two versions of the episcopal system.[24] In the one, the argument was, *episcopé* belonged to the bishop and in the other it belonged to the corporate ministry as expressed in the courts of the church. The concept of Bishop-in-Presbytery was coined, described and proposed.

The Inter-Church Relations Committee handed in its comments on the *Joint Report* to the General Assembly of 1958. The authors of the comments seem to have been reluctant to draw clear attention to the "wide variety of viewpoints" and the "many issues" on which "deep cleavages of opinion manifested themselves."[25] Differences seem to have touched upon the proposal of the Bishop-in-Presbytery. Some members had difficulty with the suggestion that the bishops should be *ex officio* members of the General Assembly. "More emphatic exception" was taken by members to the suggestion that bishops, acting collectively, should have "a necessary voice" in decisions on doctrinal and constitutional matters.[26] These objections were rooted in "a proper anxiety lest the full and final authority of the General Assembly," which was envisaged under the proposals, should nevertheless be undermined at certain points.[27] A majority of the presbyteries rejected the practical proposals of the joint report as these would affect the polity of the Church of Scotland.[28] Additional reasons for this rejection included reference to the incompatibility of the two systems of church government, the denial of the catholicity of presbyterian ministerial orders, and the fact that the supreme authority of the General Assembly was not safeguarded.[29] The General Assembly of 1959 was of the opinion that the proposals of the joint report regarding modification in the polity of the presbyterian church were unacceptable in that they implied a denial of the catholicity of the

---

[24] Report, 1957:83
[25] Report, 1958:57
[26] Report, 1958:63
[27] Report, 1958:63
[28] Report, 1959:69
[29] Report, 1959:69

Church of Scotland and of the validity and regularity of its ministry in the church catholic.[30]

In a deliverance passed in 1959, the General Assembly, besides declaring its commitment to the ecumenical movement, required that the
> next step towards greater unity between the Anglican and Presbyterian Churches lies in the recognition of one another as true members of the Church Catholic and of their ministries as valid and regular ministries of that Church.[31]

It also required that in future discussions clarity should be obtained on the meaning of unity as distinct from uniformity in church order, the meaning of "validity" as applied to ministerial orders, the meaning of the doctrine of Holy Communion, and the meaning of "the Apostolic Succession" as related to all these matters.[32] In May 1960 a committee of fifty was appointed to continue discussions on the basis outlined above.[33] The discussions were resumed in 1962.[34] As in the previous discussions, the Church of Scotland, the Presbyterian Church of England, the Church of England and the Episcopal Church of Scotland were participants. In 1963 the Church of England asked that the following issues be added to the discussions: (a) the church as royal priesthood, (b) the place of the laity in the church and (c) church, community and state.[35]

In these discussions the essential agreement between presbyterianism and episcopalianism was held onto by presbyterian participants. Concerning unity and uniformity the 1966 report concluded that there was a close connection between "Faith and Order," and that the ordained ministry was a gift of Christ to the church. Thus a measure of uniformity in church order was necessary before union could be achieved.[36] Differences between the participating churches in the forms of ordained ministry were due to historical circumstances and to different theological convictions. The report stated that these two factors "are

---

[30] Report, 1959:90
[31] Report, 1959:90
[32] Report, 1959:90
[33] Report, 1966:627
[34] Report, 1966:628
[35] Report, 1966:628-629
[36] Report, 1966:632

always intertwined and cannot be isolated from one another."[37] It was agreed that the ordained ministry in all four churches was a real gift of God to his church.[38] It was further agreed that the ordained ministry stemmed from Christ's commission to the Apostles and that no single pattern was presented in the New Testament.[39]

Concerning "validity," it was stated that the central problem arose from the fact that the Church of England and other Anglican churches "do not in practice accord full recognition to the ministry of those not ordained by a bishop standing within the historical succession."[40] In answer to the Anglican Communion, the presbyterians stated that presbyterianism maintained the essential functions of the episcopate, corporately or individually.[41] Episcopalianism and presbyterianism were contrasted as systems of church government representing differing methods of exercising oversight or *episcopé*.[42] According to the report

> the majority tradition in the Church of Scotland has regarded the corporate oversight exercised by the Presbytery as the Presbyterian equivalent of the oversight of the Bishop, and the Minister of Word and Sacrament as, in this regard, holding a place similar to that of the Anglican priest; but voices have not been wanting to suggest that the minister of Word and Sacraments holds a position analogous rather to that of the Bishop.[43]

The presbyterians agreed with the episcopal view of the office as a position representing the rule of Christ in the church.

In addition the Report described the presbyterian and Anglican views on apostolic succession. A major difference was found to exist in this area. The presbyterians considered apostolic succcesion to be the "perpetuation through history of the Apostolic faith and witness to Christ." To the Church of England, apostolic succession referred to the

---

[37] Report, 1966:632
[38] Report, 1966:632
[39] Report, 1966:633
[40] Report, 1966:635
[41] Report, 1966:638
[42] Report, 1966:638
[43] Report, 1966:640

episcopal succession in orders, by which each new bishop is consecrated by the action of other bishops through prayer and the laying-on of hands, and incorporated into the historic succession of the episcopate going back to the early days of the Church.[44]

It was explained that the one held a view on succession as succession in *function* and the other, as succession in *office*.[45]

These issues continued to receive attention both in ecumenical discussions with a view towards church union, and in Church of Scotland's consideration of its ministry. Responses from presbyteries emphasised the necessity of a mutual recognition of ministries. Some presbyteries were convined that the two systems of church government were not compatible. Others, while rejecting any form of monarchical episcopacy, felt that there was need for further and fuller consideration of the office and function of the offce of the bishop with specific reference to the value of the pastoral aspect of this office in the life of the contemporary church.[46]

In 1967 an official "Conversation" on church union in Scotland was initiated involving six Churches in Scotland: The Church of Scotland, the Episcopal Church, the Methodist Synod, the Congregational Union, the United Free Church and the Churches of Christ.[47] The *Interim Report of the Multilateral Conversation in Scotland* was presented to the General Assembly of 1972. *Baptism, Eucharist and Ministry* issued by the Faith and Order Commission of the World Council of Churches following its meeting in Lima, Peru, in January 1982, was presented to the General Assembly of 1983 with a recommendation that presbyteries consider it and send in their comments on the document.[48] *God's Reign and Our Unity*, the report of the Anglican-Reformed International Commission, 1981-1984, was published in 1984 and together with the final report of the Multilateral Conversation in Scotland, *Christian Unity - Now is the Time*, was presented to the 1985 General Assembly of the Church of

---

[44] Report, 1966:643
[45] Report, 1966:643
[46] Report, 1968:519
[47] Report, 1969:535-536
[48] Report, 1983:364

Scotland. Both reports were also referred to presbyteries for their consideration.[49]

In ecumenical discussions, consensus grew that the primary ministry was that of Christ himself,[50] that the whole church had received the commission to minister and participate in the ministry of Christ by the gift of the Holy Spirit,[51] and that the ordained ministry evolved from within the wider church as a function[52] of the church for providing leadership to the general ministry of the church.[53] According to the interim report of the Multilateral Church Conversations, the theological order that ought to govern all discussion on the role of the ordained ministry in the church must be first Christ, then the church and last the ordained ministry as derivative.[54] Within the context of these discussions a threefold ministry of bishop, presbyter and deacon was suggested as an expression of the unity which the church was seeking, and as a means of achieving that unity.[55] The bishop was defined as a minister of the Word and sacraments, who had pastoral oversight of other ministers; presbyters were to serve as pastoral ministers of the Word and sacraments in a local eucharistic community; and deacons were to represent the calling of the church as servant in the world, fulfill administrative duties and serve in elected positions of governance.[56] It was especially the non-episcopal churches that had to consider adopting this form of ministry for the sake of unity.[57] In addition there was general agreement that the guiding principles for the exercise of the ordained ministry must have a personal character providing in a specific person a focus for the unity

---

[49] Report, 1985:315, 383
[50] Report, 1972:608; *B.E.M.*, "Ministry", I:1-6; *God's Reign*, 1984:IV.73
[51] Report, 1972:608; *B.E.M.*, "Ministry", I:1-6; *God's Reign*, 1984:IV.74
[52] The Multilateral Church Conversations' Interim Report of 1972 stated twice that the ministry is not a function of the Scottish society (Report, 1972:610, 611).
[53] Report, 1972:609; *B.E.M.*, "Ministry", I:1-6; *God's Reign*, 1984:IV.77
[54] Report, 1972:610
[55] Report, 1972:608; *B.E.M.*, "Ministry", III:22, 28-31; *God's Reign*, 1984:IV.91, 92; *Christian Unity - Now is the Time*, 1985:17
[56] *B.E.M.*, "Ministry", III:28-31
[57] Report, 1986:280; *B.E.M.*, "Ministry", VI:53; *God's Reign*, 1984:IV.96; *Christian Unity - Now is the Time*, 1985:19

and witness of the community, a collegial character exercised not by one person but in shared responsibility with colleagues, and a communal character with reference to the participation of the whole church.[58]

The response from the presbyteries of the Church of Scotland to the documents of the recent ecumenical debates indicated that there was a general consensus that the ministry of the church derived from and was modelled after the ministry of Christ; that the ordained ministry was within the ministry of the whole church; and that this ministry should be exercised at local and wider levels, in personal, collegial and communal ways.[59] The responses also showed that there was a felt need for greater pastoral care of pastors, not necessarily with reference to a bishop, but of a personal nature.[60] However, the concept of a three-fold ministry, of a distinct order of bishop, presbyter and deacon, as well as the succession and ordination tied to the office of bishop was rejected by the presbyteries.[61] On the one hand, the *Reply to the Faith and Order Commission on "Baptism, Eucharist and Ministry"* complained that

> there is no recognition of the theologically more profound two-fold pattern of ministry, of Christ, as both true proclaimer of the grace of God, in word and deed and true responder to it in worship and service.[62]

On the other hand, the reasons given for rejecting the concept of a three-fold order were that it was "not scriptural, not Reformed, not compatible with Presbyterianism, not compatible with parity of ministry, not shown by history to be essential, though recognised to be an ancient tradition."[63] For example, the claim made by *God's Reign and Our Unity* that the Reformers of the sixteenth century saw themselves as re-instating the three-fold ministry in a local version (bishop, presbyter and deacon) was rejected by presbyteries "as devoid of any historical foundation."[64] Additional comments from the presbyteries on *Christian Unity - Now is*

---

[58] *B.E.M.*, "Ministry", III:24; *God's Reign*, 1984:IV.92; *Christian Unity - Now is the Time*, 1985:17
[59] Report, 1985:337
[60] Report, 1984:394; 1985:338; 1986:270; 1987:392
[61] Report, 1984:394; 1985:380; 1986:270; 1987:394
[62] Report, 1985:380
[63] Report, 1986:282
[64] Report, 1987:392

the Time gave a further impression of the differences of opinion on the offices prevalent in the Church of Scotland.

The large majority of presbyteries that commented on this report's treatment of ministries strongly criticised it on grounds of its "clericalism" or neglect of the ministry of the whole people of God, its neglect or misunderstanding of the eldership and its support of a threefold order of ministry.[65] Five presbyteries stressed the "partnership or unity or parity of ministers and elders." Three of them therefore rejected the use of the term "presbyter" to refer to the minister only, excluding elders. Several stressed the pastoral, liturgical, governmental and "episcopal" roles of elders. Support for the minister-elder partnership was found in the "single chamber nature" of courts.[66] One presbytery excused the report's neglect of eldership on the grounds that the Church of Scotland itself was unclear and divided in its understanding of it![67]

7.2 The Church of Scotland and its ministry

Amidst the ecumenical activity the need was felt for a clear statement regarding the policy of the Church of Scotland on its ministry. An overture from the presbytery of Deer to the General Assembly of 1959

> to re-examine and re-formulate the doctrine of ordination to the Holy Ministry and to re-examine and re-formulate the expression of such doctrine as it is set forth in the Act of Ordination as prescribed for use in the Courts of the Church

was referred to the Panel on Doctrine.[68] An interim report, based on the subordinate standards of the Church of Scotland, was presented to the General Assembly of 1963 for discussion by the presbyteries.[69] A finalised statement was presented to the General Assembly of 1965. The *Statement on the Ministry of Word and Sacraments* was approved by this General Assembly as "indicating the position of the Church of Scotland in

---

[65] Report, 1986:280
[66] Report, 1986:282
[67] Report, 1986:282
[68] Report, 1962:818
[69] Report, 1963:752ff

the matter."[70] Two issues which confronted the Church of Scotland in ecumenical conversations received attention, namely the question of a valid ministry and apostolic succession, as well as the relationship of the ordained minister to the local congregation and to the wider church. The Assembly of 1963 had to deal with the report on *Conversations between the Church of Scotland and the Congregationalist Union of Scotland* in which the issues of proper ordination "by those to whom it belong" and the relationship of the minister in the local congregation to the wider Church received attention.[71]

In the *Statement on the Ministry of Word and Sacraments* a reformed view on the ministry was held onto. It was stated that:

> 1. Christ is the Head of His Church and the Source of all Ministry in it.
>
> 2. To the church, as the Servant People of God, there is committed a mission and ministry to the whole world. This general ministry belongs to the whole fellowship of the church as the Body of Christ.
>
> 3. Within this general ministry of His Church, Christ calls some whom He appoints to a special ministry, for the proclamation of the Gospel, the shepherding of His People, the preservation of the purity of the Faith and the continuance of the Church under His Rule.[72]

Concerning apostolic succession the report stated that the continuance of the ministry did not depend upon the persons or ministers in their succession but upon the Word faithfully preached and the sacraments faithfully administered.[73] In opposition to Congregationalism it stated that four elements were considered necessary for lawful calling: an inner call of God, an outer calling by the church through acceptance by a presbytery which judged the person suitable in life and doctrine for the ministry, election by a congregation (or appointment to work in the

---

[70] Report, 1965:707
[71] Report, 1963:746-750
[72] Report, 1965:703
[73] Report, 1965:703

church's mission at home or abroad), and commissioning called ordination.[74] This ordination was defined as the solemn setting apart of a person to some public church office in line with the *Form of Presbyterial Church-Government*.[75] Ordination was for life, an act of the presbytery, and non-ministerial participation in ordination and in laying on of hands was not permitted.[76]

In 1982 the General Assembly instructed the Panel on Doctrine, in light of the great variety of ministries that were being exercised in the church, to clarify the church's theology of ministry in general, and in particular to offer guidance as to how these various ministries related to each other and to the ministry of the church as a whole.[77] This remittance was given to the Panel on Doctrine as a response of the Assembly to the unease expressed in the report of the Diaconate Board concerning the future role and position of the diaconate within the Church. In 1985 a report titled *Ministry. An Interim Report* was presented to the General Assembly.

Rejecting the three-fold order of ministry which was proposed in ecumenical reports, this report dealt with a new view of a two-fold concept of ministry, namely *kerygma* and *diakonia*. This two-fold ministry could be distinguished in the ministry of Christ which was "the starting point of all ministry."[78] All Christians were called to share in this continuing two-fold ministry. This "baptismal ministry" of the whole church, as the report called it, was in agreement with the insistence of the reformed tradition that faithfulness to the Gospel rather than possession of any given order or lineage is the true sign of "succession" from the apostles.[79] Besides this general "baptismal ministry" there were some who were entrusted to the particular responsibility of proclamation and service, ministries which had no existence and purpose outside the rest of the believing community.[80] Some were set apart by the church for the kerygmatic

---

[74] Report, 1965:704
[75] Report, 1965:704
[76] Report, 1965:705
[77] Report, 1983:152
[78] Report, 1985:144
[79] Report, 1985:144
[80] Report, 1985:145, 151

ministry of Word and sacraments and ordained by the laying on of hands. Their primary concern with *kerygma* did not exempt them from the demands of *diakonia*.[81]

The second special ministry identified within "the baptismal ministry of all" was that to which the church commissioned some to take the lead in the servanthood of the church and to encourage the obedient response of all the people to God's Word of grace. Their primary concern with *diakonia* did not exempt them from the task of *kerygma*.[82] The panel stated that it was not true that those whom the early church in Acts 6 appointed to care for its widows were called "deacons" as if *diakonia* consisted only of material alms-giving, or that those who literally served the tables were the sole *diakonoi* (deacons). On the contrary, those who were not chosen for this duty but gave themselves to prayer and proclamation continued in "the diakonia of the Word" (Acts 6:4). Diaconal service, according to the panel, was the calling and lifestyle of the whole church which received the "service of reconciliation" (2 Cor. 5:18).[83]

The panel appreciated the emphasis of the present day church on all Christians being servants and stewards in the image of Christ's *diakonia*. The panel stated that therefore

> it is a truth no longer to be obscured, if it once was, by the decision of the later New Testament church to designate some rather than others in the fellowship as 'deacons' still less by the fact that history had sometimes subordinated 'deacons' in the Church of Scotland to the temporal concerns of finance and fabric.[84]

The marginalisation and de-spiritualisation of *diakonia* had to be reversed. It was suggested that the best way to do this was to re-appropriate the fact that the New Testament deacons received a "spiritual calling, to assist those responsible for worship and to help the community to respond to the gospel with the 'liturgy' of concrete sacrifice and service."[85]

---

[81] Report, 1985:152
[82] Report, 1985:145
[83] Report, 1985:155
[84] Report, 1985:155
[85] Report, 1985:155

According to the panel, the Church of Scotland already had a "Diaconate" commissioned by the church to full-time exercise of this complementary "ministry of service," but it must be concretely associated with the ministry of Word and sacraments.[86] This ministry should, therefore, take its place amid the structures of orderly leadership as full members of the kirk session of the congregations to which they were attached, and of the presbyteries within whose bounds they served.[87]

The panel did not relate this discussion on the ministry of diakonia to the traditional office of the deacon. Instead they related it to the elder of the church. The panel was convinced that the New Testament "presbyter" was analogous to preachers and pastors in the ministry of the Word and sacraments, and that the elders of the Church of Scotland corresponded more closely to the deacons who assisted both in worship and in directing congregational care and witness.[88] This closely resembled the Anglican practice of the deacon as an assistant to the bishop. The identifying of the office of the elder with that of the New Testament "presbyter" by the *Second Book of Discipline* contributed to the fact that the eldership came to be associated less with *diakonia* in the imitation of Christ than with power and rule on the model of the state.[89] And, in the view of the panel, "to this day the problem remains of determining what elders are."[90]

The panel suggested that within the structures of the church the present diaconate should be linked with the eldership. The traditional link of the eldership with the ministry of the Word and sacraments would be re-affirmed, rather than denied, by designating the eldership as a "ministry of service".[91] The eldership should be more involved in the regular worship services of the congregations, thus reflecting the relation between *kerygma* and *diakonia*. They should also receive authority to

---

[86] Report, 1985:155
[87] Report, 1985:156
[88] Report, 1985:156
[89] Report, 1985:156
[90] Report, 1985:156
[91] Report, 1985:157

preside at the Table where such a need arises (house communions were mentioned).[92]

Two clusters of ministry were suggested to serve the twofold ministry of Christ. To the first cluster of Word and sacraments would belong the ordained ministers of the Word and sacraments, full and part-time non-stipendiary auxiliary ministers and those entering probation. With them may be associated lay missionaries and readers. To the second cluster of the ministry of service would belong the diaconate and the eldership and any others whose service the Church wished formally to recognise.[93]

Responses of presbyteries to the interim report were not altogether positive towards its proposals. The majority felt that the distinction between Christ's ministry of *kerygma* and *diakonia* was not a helpful way to describe the ministry of Christ.[94] All presbyteries who answered the questions replied in the affirmative that the ministry of the Church begins not with the ordained but with the calling of the whole people of God. As to implimentation, the most common comment was that leadership was needed from both ministers and elders, and that training and education should be given to prevent the church being so minister-centred that the ministry is left in the hands of a few.[95] Those presbyteries which were unhappy with the twofold division of Christ's ministry also had reservations about the distinction being applied to the ministries of the church. One objection was that the function of "ruling" in relation to the eldership was not given enough emphasis and that the role of the diaconate should be spelled out since not many in the church were aware of its position.[96] It was thought inconsistent that the elder should preside at the sacrament while belonging to the other cluster, and that the diaconate should be left out of consideration in relation to celebration.[97] Most presbyteries reacted favourably to the suggestion that under certain circumstances the Lord's Supper could be

---

[92] Report, 1985:157
[93] Report, 1985:159-160
[94] Report, 1988:135
[95] Report, 1988:135
[96] Report, 1988:136
[97] Report, 1988:136

administered by lay missionaries, readers and elders.[98] The majority of the presbyteries which replied wished to retain ordination for the eldership and to change the commissioning of the diaconate to ordination.[99]

The panel presented the first part of its final report, *Ministry: A Theological Perspective*, to the Assembly of 1988. In light of the comments on the interim report of 1985, the panel presented a revised theological description of the ministry of the church. The emphasis was now on the mission and ministry of the church as grounded in God's own mission to the world, with the pattern of the Trinity - the loving community of Father, Son and Holy Spirit - the fundamental pattern for all ministry within the church.[100] The sending of the Spirit and the sending of the church in the power of the Spirit, it was explained, were located within the sending of Christ and in his obedience to the will of the Father, and the ministry in the church must be characterised by the humiliation and exaltation of Christ.[101] Since the congregation was the concrete setting for the ministry of the whole people, the report questioned the practice of the "ministry" being associated with one person.[102] From the early days of the church, the report continued, direction and leadership were given to the baptised by those to whom specific tasks were designated. The nature of this ministry must reflect the pattern of Christ's own ministry. It must be leadership in fellowship, a corporate leadership.[103] It meant that power structures of privilege and of rule were not appropriate models of leadership. The pattern of Christ's leadership, the report continued, was one which encourages the responsibility and responsiveness of the whole people through promoting the gifts of togetherness and

---

[98] Report, 1988:136
[99] Report, 1988:136
[100] Report, 1989:191
[101] Report, 1989:191
[102] Report, 1989:192
[103] Report, 1989:192; The General Assembly of 1985, in response to *BEM*, resolved that the Church's structure must be examined to see whether the communal, the collegial, and especially the personal dimension of oversight are adequately discharged (Report, 1985:312).

friendship.[104] The report concluded that in the Church of Scotland the basis of this kind of corporate leadership is found in the session of the congregation and also in the corporate leadership of the presbytery, synod and general assembly.[105] In order to spell out the pattern of leadership in the church today the report laid down that the structure of the church's ministries must be flexible to allow for change and reform. They must also reflect the biblical pattern of proclamation, worship and service.[106]

In 1989 the rest of the report on the ministries of the Church was presented to the General Assembly. According to the report, within the ministry of the whole people of God, gifts of Christ for leading and encouraging were being expressed in the Church of Scotland in the following ministries: the ministry of the Word and sacrament, the ministry of the eldership, and the ministry of the diaconate.[107]

The ministry of the Word and sacraments in the church was considered to be in accordance with the gospel writers' belief that it was the will of Christ that individuals within the church should have direct responsibility for preaching, celebration, teaching and pastoral care.[108] It was argued that the biblical pattern of this leadership, integrated in the church, allowed for no suggestion of a hierarchy within the fellowship.[109] This ministry of the Word and sacraments was given by God, and was not an arrangement devised by the church. The tasks of this ministry were assumed to be preaching, administering the sacraments and nurturing the flock through teaching and pastoral care.[110] Appointment to this ministry was by ordination. Three separate but related elements were involved in a candidate's ordination to the ministry of the Word and sacraments: i) The church's ratification of the individual's sense of being called; ii) A service of worship including prayer and the laying on of hands by those who were already ordained; iii) A specific sphere of

---

[104] Report, 1989:192
[105] Report, 1989:192
[106] Report, 1989:192
[107] Report, 1989:193
[108] Report, 1989:193
[109] Report, 1989:193
[110] Report, 1989:194

service.[111] The concept of an linear apostolic succession in the ordained ministry was rejected by the report.[112] Each ordination and each ministry was considered to be a new act of grace from the Head of the church - grace conferred through those who already stood within it, but not conjured up by their pedigree.[113] An apostolic church was described as a church true to the faith of the apostles.[114] The panel included under the ministry of the Word and sacraments non-parochial ministries, licentiates, readers and auxiliary ministers, and leaders of house groups.[115]

As in the case of the 1986 *Interim Report* the choice was made for the "lay" theory of the eldership being assistants to the presbyterate and more in line with the New Testament deacon.[116] The task of the eldership was the diaconal ministry of leading the people in their worship, prompting their response to the gospel and seeking the fruit of it in the life and mission of the whole Church.[117] The common ground between the eldership and the diaconate of the church was considered to be carrying out the same enabling task but in different ways.[118] The panel, however, was not convinced that all was well with the eldership. It proposed, therefore, to revitalise it by education, popular election and the removal of the practice of ordination.[119] The report finally pleaded for the incorporation of the diaconate, which developed in the Church of Scotland since the 1880s and is at present considered to be a distinct office, into the courts of the church.[120]

Reaction from presbyteries to the report was directed mainly at the report's view of the eldership. Some presbyteries saw no reason why the eldership appeared to have been singled out as the only form of ministry

---

[111] Report, 1989:195
[112] Report, 1989:195
[113] Report, 1989:195
[114] Report, 1989:195-6
[115] Report, 1989:196-7
[116] Report, 1989:199-200
[117] Report, 1989:200
[118] Report, 1989:200
[119] Report, 1989:200-202
[120] Report, 1989:203-204

to be under consideration for change. Most considered the panel to have been far to radical. Some suspected undisclosed and sinister ecumenical motives. Some thought presbyterianism itself would be under threat if the Church followed Knox's guidelines rather than Melville's - "the office (of the ruling elder) being a continuing one, handed on from the Apostolic Church." The consensus of twenty-eight presbyteries out of thirty replies were firmly for no change.[121] One justification frequently repeated in favour of an ordained and life-long eldership was that it acted as a brake on the power of the minister.[122] The panel drew attention to the observation of the presbytery of Glasgow to this kind of statement: "If the eldership is a safeguard against ministerial clericalism, care must be taken to ensure that the eldership itself does not become a remote self-perpetuating ruling class within the Church."[123]

Twentieth century Church of Scotland, in its involvement in ecumenical discussions and in reconsidering its offices, faced the consequences of the inability of presbyterianism to come to terms with episcopalianism with regard to the place and function of the offices and their mutual inter-relationship in the church. A variety of opinions were expressed reflecting that no reformed theology on the offices developed in Scottish presbyterian ecclesiology. Presbyterian participants to ecumenical discussions found it possible to agree to the re-introduction of the bishop as a prelude to church union and to hold onto the two-fold episcopal concept of the ministry, namely, the bishop or presbyter and deacon. In the same way it was possible for the Panel on Doctrine to avoid the participation of the elder in the government of the church and to promote the two-fold order of the ministry. Considerations on the diaconate of the church were dealt with without any reference to the traditional Scottish reformed deacon. Reactions to an episcopal approach were in accordance with the conviction of the government of the church by presbyters in assembly. This did not necessarily mean agreement on the place and function of the offices in the church and their relationship with one another. Parity of the offices of the minister, the elder and the deacon was not considered.

---

[121] Report, 1990:195
[122] Report, 1990:196
[123] Report, 1990:196

CHAPTER 8

CONCLUSION

Scottish reformed ecclesiology - fundamental to church offices - was all along conditioned by a specific ecclesiastical and political context. The process followed in reforming the Church of Scotland made for the development of a typical Scottish ecclesiology and conception of its ministry.

The initial concern of the Scottish reformers was, in accordance with Calvin's model, to establish a vital active, confessing church with the worship service at its centre. In line with Calvin's teaching the emphasis was on the local church as fellowship of believers which must possess the true marks of the church. The earliest Scottish reformation documents explained these marks to be the preaching of the Word, the administration of the sacraments, and the exercise of discipline. Convinced of the scriptural support for Calvin's model, the Scottish reformers did not enter into a renewed scriptural justification for their reformation programme once it became possible to reform the existing Church of Scotland. They, however, had to consider the reformation of an established national episcopal church with its constituted and integrated parishes and tradition. This required the adaptation of the Genevan model. The adaptation of the Genevan model in Scotland was conditioned by the specific political and ecclesiastical context and a typical Scottish "common sense" approach to deal with problems in which episcopal elements were retained. The initial concern for the local church as visible community of faith and institution, with its centre in the worship service, in which Christ rules through His Word and Spirit using office-bearers and the means of grace – thus complete church and local manifestation of the universal church – was at an early stage overshadowed by a concern for the national church as overall and integrated institution representing the universal church. Church politically the visible church as living community of faith ruled by Christ through

Word and Spirit using office bearers from an early date received attention only in so far it was related to a general organization of the national church and not as an integral part of a reformed ecclesiological departure point. The starting point in Scottish reformed ecclesiology shifted from the visible church as community of faith *and* as institution to the visible church institution representing the universal church.

The growing ecclesiological shift to a one-sided emphasis on the church as institution was encouraged by the answer to the question as to who shares the authority of the church and how to secure that authority. The emphasis fell on the church as an institution distinct from the state. Melville could not accept the reconciliation of the episcopal system with the system Calvin shaped. Practically it opened the way for state control of the church. A choice had to be made for either presbyters or bishops. The solution was found in the replacement of the episcopal hierarchy with a hierarchy of presbyters in assembly. The episcopal transfer of the government of Christ to man – through the single presbyter was maintained – as government by presbyters in assembly. *The Second Book of Discipline* represented a more consistent merging of reformed church polity with episcopacy. The district eldership that would become the presbytery was adopted and described. This regional organisation consisting of presbyters who were representatives of the local congregations replaced the bishop and his diocese and prepared the way for the separation of the office of the minister from the local congregation.

In their struggle against the rule of the bishop and state interference in matters of the church, English Puritans and Scottish Presbyterians had to face parliamentary Erastians and Independentism. In reaction, and in line with the *Second Book of Discipline*, the emphasis fell on the church as constituted institution with authority vested in official assemblies. The Westminster Assemblies defined an all inclusive and comprehensive presbyterianism scholastically by a confession of faith, a larger and smaller catechism, a directory for public worship and a form of church government. A system of church government in which the church was considered in term of a constituted institution was maintained and ruled, and scripturally as well as confessionally reasoned. The replacement of the rule of Christ in the local church through His Word and Spirit using office-bearers by substituted representation of offices in the assembly was held onto.

With the Westminster Assembly the adaptation of the Scottish episcopal system to the scriptural and reformed conviction of the church in the process of establishing a national reformed church was completed. Presbyterianism as adapted episcopalianism is evident - *episcopé* related to an individual in hierarchy was replaced by *episcopé* exercised by presbyters in hierarchical assemblies or courts. The authority of the church was centralised in the highest or general assembly. A clericalistic approach to the office of the minister, in accordance with Puritan episcopalianism, was confirmed. The separation of the office of the minister from the local congregation was completed. The minister was now to hold his position by virtue of the presbytery. The offices of the elder and deacon were formally reduced to assistants of the office of the minister.

The pattern for future ecclesiological consideration was established. Common to the Moderates and the Evangelicals in their approach to maintain the spiritual independence of the church was the ecclesiological emphasis on the church as an institution and the neglect of the offices of minister, elder and deacon as distinct ministries in the church. Nineteenth and early twentieth century restructuring of presbyterianism emphasized the uniting of separated church institutions accompanied by a progressive erosion of the Westminster Confession of Faith. The concern remained for the institution without the necessary consideration for the faith community. This became a characteristic of twentieth century discussions on church unity. A major difficulty was reconciling the various conceptions of the offices in the church.

An important contributing factor to the inability of Scottish presbyterianism to arrive at a theology of the ministry of the reformed offices is the specific departure point of Scottish presbyterian ecclesiology. The presbyterial-synodical system of church government takes as its departure point the rule of Christ through His Word and Spirit using office-bearers in the visible church. Both aspects of the visible church – the church as institution *and* as community of faith - must be taken seriously. In Scottish presbyterianism ecclesiology the church as institution was separated from the church as community of faith.

Due to practical considerations (e.g. the decisive struggle for the autonomy of the church against state control) and an unscriptural pragmatical approach in dealing with issues the church as institution became the starting point of all church political considerations. Ecclesiology was separated from christology and pneumatology. Neither in the formative documents of presbyterianism, nor the different traditions that developed in the Scottish reformed church was the work of the Holy Spirit in maintaining the rule of Christ through His Word using office-bearers considered in terms of the government of the church. As a result the rule of Christ was replaced by that of man and the church was considered as an institution to be governed in accordance with its constitution and enacted laws. By neglecting the rule of Christ through both His Word and Spirit, Scottish presbyterianism degenerated into a comprehensive ecclesiasticism. In this approach to church government in which the power of the keys were constantly considered in terms of *postestas* and not *diakonia* no room was left for the development of the offices as ministries to serve the rule of Christ through His Word and Spirit.

Parity of the reformed offices was not considered. In accordance with an episcopal conception the offices were considered in terms of rank and dignity. The priority of the office of the minister was held onto. The conviction of the lower offices being assistants to the higher offices, and that what can be done by the lower offices can be done by the higher because the higher possesses the power of the lower, prevented the development of the offices of elder and deacon as ministries in their own right. The wide range of opinions on the offices in the Church of Scotland in light of twentieth century ecumenical conversations and this Church's own desire to improve its ministry confirms the incomplete development of Scottish presbyterian ecclesiology in the area of the ministry of the offices in the church.

The development of Scottish reformed ecclesiology, though acknowledging the Headship of Christ over His church, reflects the consistent result of man's taking into hand the rule of Christ, and is a powerful reminder that the church is called to constantly reconsider its ministry in terms of the ministry of Christ through His Word and the Holy Spirit. It has been pointed out that whenever the church neglects the confession of the Lordship of Christ or does not consider the relationship between Christ and the church in the correct manner, it is immediately reflected in the polity of the church.[1] This happened in the Church of Scotland where the office of the minister was separated from the congregation in a clericalistic sense, the offices of the elders reduced to assistants of the minister, and the authority of Christ transferred to the offices which govern the church through courts in an episcopal sense.

The presbyterian system of church government became characteristic of the government of the Reformed churches in Central Africa. In these churches the emphasis falls on the maintenance of the institution through its executive functionaries in accordance with a comprehensive law book. The local church as *locus* for the direct rule of Christ enjoys little or no attention. The cause is found in the Scottish presbyterian church polity uncritically accepted by the Dutch Reformed missionaries and uncritically maintained by the Africa church. From this overview of the political development of the Scottish presbyterian church the necessity for a continuous evaluation of the ministry of the offices in terms of the ministry of Christ and its Reformed confirmation is clear.

---

[1] Jonker, 1965:4

BIBLIOGRAPHY

Ainslee JL 1940. *The Doctrine of Ministerial Order in the Reformed Churches of the 16th and 17th Centuries.* Edinburgh: T&T Clark.

Ainslee JL 1944. "The Scottish Reformed Church and English Puritanism," in *Records of the Scottish Church History Society*, viii:75-95. Glasgow.

Avis PDL 1981. *The Church in the Theology of the Reformers.* London: Marshall Morgan and Scott.

Baillie Robert 1645. *A Dissuasive from the Errours of the Time: Wherein the Tenets of the Principal Sects, especially of the Independents, are drawn together in one Map, for the most part, in the words of their own Authours, and their maine principles are examined by the Touch-Stone of the Holy Scriptures.* Published by Authority. London: Published for Samuel Gellibrand at the Brasen Serpent in Pauls Church-Yard.

Baillie Robert 1646. *An Historical Vindication of the Government of the Church of Scotland.* London: Published for Samuel Gellibrand at the Brasen Serpent in Pauls-Churchyard.

Baillie Robert 1841. *The Letters and Journals of Robert Baillie*, A.M. Principal of the University of Glasgow. MDCXXXVII-MDCLXII. Volume Second. Edited by David Laing. Edinburgh: Robert Ogle.

Balfour Paul Sir James 1912. "The Post-Reformation Elder," in *Scottish Historical Review*, ix:253-262. Glasgow.

Bannerman James 1868a. *The Church of Christ. Treatise on the Nature, Powers, Ordinances, Discipline, and Government of the Christian Church, vol. I.* Edited by his son. Edinburgh: T&T Clark.

Bannerman James 1868b. *The Church of Christ. Treatise on the Nature, Powers, Ordinances, Discipline, and Government of the Christian Church, vol. II.* Edited by his son. Edinburgh: T&T Clark.

Baptism, Eucharist and Ministry 1982. Faith and Order paper no. 111. World Council of Churches, Geneva.

Barbour GF [1934]. *The Elder and His Work.* Prepared at the request of The Central Council of the Church of Scotland Elders' and Office-bearers' Union.

Bavinck H 19766. *Gereformeerd Dogmatiek. Vol. 4.* Kampen: Uitgeversmaatschappij JH Kok.

Bayne Peter 1893. *The Free Church of Scotland. Her Origen, Founders, and Testimony.* Edinburgh: T&T Clark.

Benton W Wilson JR 1969. *The Ecclesiology of George Hill, 1750-1819.* Unpublished Ph. D. Thesis. New College, Faculty of Divinity, University of Edinburgh, Edinburgh.

Berkhof H 19733. *Christelijk Geloof.* Nijkerk: Uitgeverij GF Callenbach.

Beveridge H 1962. *Institution of the Christian Religion.* Grand Rapids: Eerdmans Publishing House.

Beveridge W 1904. *A Short History of the Westminster Assembly.* Edinburgh: T&T Clark.

Blair William 1888. *The United Presbyterian Church. A Handbook of its History and Principles.* Edinburgh: Andrew Elliot.

Boon R 1965. *Apostolische ambt en reformatie. Primair probleem der oecumene.* Nijkerk: Uitgeverij GF Callenbach.

Bouwman H 1928. *Gereformeerd Kerkrecht. Eerste Deel.* Kampen: Kok.

Bouwman H 1934. *Gereformeerd Kerkrecht. Tweede Deel. Het Recht der kerken in de Practijk.* Kampen: Kok

Bronkhorst AJ 1947. *Schrift en Kerkorde. Een bijdrage tot het onderzoek naar de mogelijkheid van een "Schriftuurlijke Kerkorde."* Den Haag: Zuid-Holl. Boek-en Handelsdrukkerij.

Brown Callum G 1987. *The Social History of Religion in Scotland since 1730.* London: Methuen.

Brown E 1991. "Die hervertolking van die paradigma in verband met die Kollegialisme om die Afrikaanse kerke kerkregtelik te verstaan," in *Hervormde Teologiese Studies,* 48:691-715.

Brown KM 1989. "In search of the Godly Magistrate," in *Journal of Ecclesiastical History,* 40:553-581.

Brown Steward 1982. *Thomas Chalmers and the Godly Commonwealth.* Oxford: Oxford University Press.

Brown Thomas 1891. *Church and State in Scotland. A Narrative of the Struggle for Independence from 1560-1843.* The Third of the Chalmers Lectures. Edinburgh: Machiven and Wallas.

Brown Thomas 1893. *Annals of the Disruption: with extracts from the narratives of ministers who left the Scottish Establishment in 1843.* Edinburgh: MacNiven and Wallace.

Buchanan Robert 1845. *The Ten Years Conflict: Being the History of the Church of Scotland, Vol. 1.* Glasgow: Blackie and Son.

Bulloch James 1991. *The Scots Confession of 1560. A Modern Translation.* Edinburgh: The Saint Andrew Press.

Burleigh JHS 1949. "The Presbyter in Presbyterianism," in *Scottish Journal of Theology,* 2:293-316.

Burleigh JHS 1960. *A Church History of Scotland.* London: Oxford University Press.

Burn-Murdoch H 1939. *Presbytery and Apostolic Succession.* London: Student Christian Movement Press.
Calderwood David 1842. *The History of the Kirk of Scotland.* Ed. Thomas Thompson (Volumes i-vii) and David Laing (Vol.viii). Edinburgh: Printed for the Wodrow Society.
Cameron James K 1972. *The First Book of Discipline, with Introduction and Commentary.* Edinburgh: St. Andrew Press.
Campbell James J 1930. *Two Centuries of the Church of Scotland, 1707-1929.* Paisley: Alexander Gardner Ltd.
Campbell Peter Colin 1866. *The Theory of the Ruling Eldership or the Position of the Lay Ruler in the Reformed Church Examined.* Edinburgh: William Blackwood and Sons.
Campbell WM 1958. *The Triumph of Presbyterianism.* Edinburgh: The Saint Andrew Press.
Carruthers SW 1938. "The Solemn League and Covenant: Its Text and Its Translations, " in *Records of the Scottish Church History Society,* vi:262-251.
[Cartwright Thomas 1644] *A Directory of Church-Government. Anciently contended for, and as farre as the Times would suffer, practiced by the first Non-conformists in the dais of Queen Elizabeth, Found in the study by the most accomplished Divine, Mr. Thomas Cartwright, after his death and reserved to be published for such a time as this. Published by Authority.* London: John Wright.
Charteris AH 1905. *The Church of Christ. Its Life and Work.* London: Macmillan and Co. Ltd.
Cheyne AC 1963. "The Westminster Standards: A Century of Re-appraisal," in *Records of the Scottish Church History Society,* xiv:199-214. Glasgow.
Chitnis Anand C 1976. *The Scottish Enlightenment. A Social History.* London: Croom Helm.
Clark Ivo M 1929. *A History of Church Discipline in Scotland.* Aberdeen: W&W Lindsay.
Chocrane Thomas 1885. *Handbook and Index to the Principal Acts of the Assembly of the Free Church of Scotland, 1843-1885.* Second Edition.
Coertzen P 1991a. *Gepas en Ordelik. 'n Teologiese verantwoording van die Orde vir en van die Kerk.* Pretoria: RGN-Uitgewers.
Coertzen Pieter 1991b. "Presbyterial Church Government. Ius Divinum, Ius Ecclesiasticum or Ius Humanum," in *Calvin Erbe und Auftrag. Festschrift für Wilhelm Neuser zu seinem 65 Geburtstag, 329-342.* Herausgegeben von Willem van't Spijker. Kampen: Kok Pharos Publishing House.
Cooper James 1907: *The Elder: The Nature of his office, and his opportunities of usefulness in the present day.* An address delivered to the Church of Scotland Office-bearers' Association of the Presbytery of Dundee. Dundee: John Leng & Co. Ltd.

Couper WJ 1925. "The Reformed Church in Scotland, its Congregations, Ministers and Students," in *Records of the Scottish Church History Society,* II:160f.f. Edinburgh

A Course for Elders (1963-1964). 2 Volumes, Edinburgh: Commission on Adult Education.

Cox James T (ed) 1934. *Practice and Procedure in the Church of Scotland.* Edinburgh: William Blackwood and Sons

Cox James T (ed) 1976. *Practice and Procedure in the Church of Scotland.* 6th Edition edited by Rev. F.F.M. MacDonald. Publiashed by the Committee on General Administration. The Church of Scotland.

Christian Unity – Now is the Time, The Multilateral Church Conversations in Scotland Report. 1985. Edinburgh: The Saint Andrew Press.

Cronjé JM 1958. *Die Selfstandigwording van die Bantoekerk. Met spesiale verwysing na die Nederduitse Gereformeerde Sendingkerk in Noord-Rhodesië.* Ongepubliseerde proefskrif ingehandig ter verkryging van die graad DOCTOR PHILOSOPHIAE aan die Universiteit van die Oranje-Vrystaat, Bloemfontein, Suid-Afrika.

Cunningham John 1882. *The Church History of Scotland. Vol II.* Second Edition. Edinburgh: James Thin.

Cunningham William 1868. *Discussions on Church Principles: Popish, Erastian and Presbyterian.* Edited by his literary executors. Edinburgh: T&T Clark.

D'Assonville, VE 1968. *John Knox and the Institutes of Calvin.* Durban: Drakensberg Press Limited.

Davies A Mervyn 1965. *Presbyterian Heritage. Switzerland, Great Britain, America.* Atlanta: John Knox Press.

De Witt JR 1969. *Jus Divinum. The Westminster Assembly and the Divine Right of Church Government.* Kampen: Kok.

Dickenson William Croft(ed) 1946. *John Knox's History of the Reformation in Scotland. Vol. One and Two.* Thomas Nelson and Sons Ltd. Edinburgh, London

Dickson David 1871. *The Elder and His Work.* Edinburgh: Andrew Elliot & John Maclaren.

Donald Peter H 1990.*'Anent the ministry of the eldership': An aspect of reformation in the Church of Scotland.* Dissertation submitted to the Departments of Christian Ethics en Practical Theology and of Ecclesiastical History towards the degree of B.D. Honours. New College, University of Edinburgh, Edinburgh.

Donaldson G 1945. "The Scottish Episcopate at the Reformation," in *English Historical Review,* lx:349-364. London: Longmans, Green and Co.

Donaldson G 1955. "The Polity of the Scottish Church, 1560-1600," in *Records of the Scottish Church History Society,* xi:212-216. Glasgow.

Donaldson G 1960. *The Scottish Reformation.* Cambridge: The University Press.
Donaldson G 1972. *Scotland. Church and Nation through Sixteen Centuries.* Second Edition. Edinburgh: Scottish Academic Press.
Donaldson G 1984. *Scottish Historical Documents.* Edinburgh: Scottish Academic Press.
Donaldson G 1990. *The Faith of the Scots.* London: BT Batsford LTD.
Douglas JD 1964. *The Light of the North. The Story of the Scottish Covenanters.* Grand Rapids: Wm.B. Eerdmans.
Doyle P 1930. "Church and State and the Jure Divino Theory of Episcopacy in the English Church," in *The Church Quarterly Review,* cix:239-261. London: SPCK.
Drummond AL and J Bullock 1973. *The Scottish Church 1688-1843. The Age of the Moderates.* Edinburgh: The Saint Andrew Press.
Drummond AL and J Bullock 1975. *The Church in Victorian Scotland 1834-1874.* Edinburgh: The Saint Andrew Press.
Drummond AL and James Bullock, 1978. *The Church in Late Victorian Scotland 1834-1874.* Edinburgh: The Saint Andrew Press.
Dunlop A Ian 1959. "The Polity of the Scottish Church, 1600-1637," in *Records of the Scottish Church History Society,* xii:161-184. Glasgow.
Dunlop A Ian 1959. "The General Session. A Controversy of 1720," in *Records of the Scottish Church History Society,* xiii:223-239. Glasgow.
Dunlop A Ian 1959. "The Paths to Reunion in 1929," in *Records of the Scottish Church History Society,* xii:223-239. Glasgow.
Fleming JR 1927. *A History of the Church in Scotland 1843-1875.* Edinburgh: T&T Clark.
Fleming JR 1933. *A History of the Church in Scotland 1875-1929.* Edinburgh: T&T Clark.
Forbes Robert 1869. *Digest of Rules and Procedure in the Inferior Courts of the Free Church of Scotland. With an Appendix.* Third Edition. Edinburgh: Johnstone Hunter.
Foster Walter Roland 1958. *Bishop and Presbytery. The Church of Scotland 1661-1688.* London: SPCK.
Foster Walter Roland 1966. "The Operation of Presbyteries in Scotland," in *Records of the Scottish Church History Society,* xvi:21-33. Glasgow.
Foster Walter Roland 1975. *The Church before the Covenants. The Church of Scotland 1596-1638.* Edinburgh. Scottish Academic Press.
Gillespie George 1641. *An Assertion of the Government of the Church of Scotland in the Points of Ruling Elders, and of the Authority of Presbyters and Synods.* Edinburgh: Robert Ogle and Oliver Boyd, 1946. (Reprinted from the Edition of 1641.)

Gillespie George 1846. *Notes of Debates and Proceedings of The Assembly of Divines and Other Commissioners at Westminster.* Edited by David Meeks. Edinburgh: Robert Ogle and Boyd.

[Gillespie George] 1647. *A Form of Church Government and Ordination of Ministers contained in CXI Propositions propounded to the late General Assembly at Edinburgh.* Drawn up by George Gillespie. London.

God's Reign & Our Unity 1984. The Report of the Anglican-Reformed International Commission. London: SPCK.

Glover Janet R 1960. *The Story of Scotland.* London: Faber and Faber.

Gordon Arthur 1912. *Life of Archibald Hamilton Charteris.* London: Hodder and Stoughton.

[Guthrie James] 1690. *A Treatise of Ruling Elders and Deacons.* Revised and Published by order of the General Meeting of the Ministers and Elders of the Church. Edinburgh.

Hamilton Ian 1990. *The Erosion of Calvinist Orthodoxy. Seceders and Subscription in Scottish Presbyterianism.* Edinburgh: Rutherford House Books.

Hall David W and Joseph H Hall (Eds) 1994. *Paradigms in Polity. Classic Readings in Reformed and Presbyterian Church Government.* Grand Rapids: William B. Eerdmans Publishing Company.

[Henderson Alexander 1641]. *The Government and Order of the Church of Scotland.* Edinbourgh.

Henderson Alexander 1644. *Reformation of Church-Government in Scotland, cleered from some mistakes and Prejudices, by the Commissioners of the General Assembly of the Church of Scotland now [The Westminster Assembly] at London.* Printed for Robert Bostock, duelling in Pauls Church Yard ate the Signe of the King's Head.

Henderson GD 1935. *The Scottish Ruling Elder.* London: James Clark Limited.

Henderson GD 1937. *Religious Life in Seventeenth-Century Scotland.* Cambridge: University Press.

Henderson GD 1951a. The Claims of the Church of Scotland. Warwick: Hodder and Stoughton.

Henderson GD 1951b. *Church and Ministry. A Study in the Scottish Experience.* London: Hodder and Stoughton.

Henderson GD 1954. *Presbyterianism.* Aberdeen: The University Press.

Henderson GD 1957. *The Burning Bush. Studies in Scottish Church History.* Edinburgh. The Saint Andrew Press.

Henderson GD n.d. *Women in Eldership.* Edinburgh.

Henderson Robert W 1962. *The Teaching Office in the Reformed Tradition. A History of the Doctrinal Ministry.* Philadelphia: The Westminster Press.

Herron Andrew 1985. *The Kirk by Divine Right. Church and State: Peaceful Co-existence.* The Baird Lectures 1985. Edinburgh: The Saint Andrew Press.

Herzog Frederick 1966. "Diakonia in Modern Times, Eighteenth - Twentieth Centuries," in *Service in Christ. Essay in Honour of Karl Barth on his 80th Birthday.* Edited by James McCord and THL Parker. London. Epworth Press, 135-150.

Hethrington WM 1890. *History of the Westminster Assembly of Divines.* Fifth Edition. Edinburgh: James Gemmel.

Heyns JA 1977. *Die Kerk.* Pretoria: NG Kerkboekhandel.

Highet John 1950. *The Churches in Scotland Today. A survey of their principles, strength, work and statement.* Glasgow: Jackson son & Company.

Hill Ninian 1919. *The Story of the Scottish Church from the Earliest Times.* Glasgow: James Maclehose and Sons.

Innes Alexander Taylor 1867. *The Law of Creeds in Scotland. A Treatise on the Legal Relation of Churches in Scotland Established and not Established, to their Doctrinal Confessions.* London: William Blackwood.

Jonker WD 1965. *Om die Regering van Christus en Sy Kerk.* Pretoria: UNISA.

Jonker WD 1970. *Als een Riet in de Wind ... Gedachten naar aanleiding van de huidige discussie rondom het ambt.* Kampen: Kok.

King David 1844. *The Ruling Eldership of the Christian Church.* Edinburgh: Willam Oliphant and Sons.

King David 1846. *The Ruling Eldership of the Christian Church.* 2nd Edition. Edinburgh: Willam Oliphant and Sons.

Kirby Ethyn Williams 1964. "The English Presbyterians in the Westminster Assembly," in *Church History,* xxxiii:418-427. The American Society of Church History.

Kirk James (ed) 1980. *The Second Book of Discipline. With Introduction and Commentary.* Edinburgh: The Saint Andrew Press.

Kirk James 1983. "Royal and Lay Patronage in the Jacobean Kirk, 1572-1600," in *Church, Politics and Society. Scotland 1408-1929.* Edited by Norman MacDougall, Edinburgh: John Donald Publishers.

Kirk James 1989. *Patterns of Reform. Continuity and Change in the Reformation of the Kirk.* Edinburgh: T&T Clark.

Kleynhans EPJ 1981. *Gereformeerde Kerkreg. Deel 1: Inleiding.* Pretoria: NG Kerkboekhandel.

Laing David (ed) 1855. *The Works of John Knox; Collected and Edited by David Laing. Six volumes.* Edinburgh: Thomas George Stevenson.

Lachman David C 1988. *The Marrow Controversy 1718-1723. AM Historical and Theological Analysis.* Edinburgh: Rutherford House.

Lamb John A 1958. "The Kalender of the Books of Comone Order: 1564-1644," in *Records of the Scottish Church History Society,* xii:15-28. Glasgow.

Lake Peter and Maria Dowling 1987. *Protestantism and the National Church in Sixteenth Century England.* London: Croom Helm.

Leishman T 1895. "Neglected Provisions and Remediable Defects in the Presbyterian Organisation, and its Better Adaptation to Existing Needs," in *Scottish Church Society Conferences, Second Series: Vol II: The Divine Life of the Church. An Affirmation of the Doctrine of Baptism with contributions relating to the Scottish Church, her History, Work, and Present need,* 48-58. Edinburgh: J. Gardner Hitt

Leishman JF 1909 "Adequate Security for the Continuance of the Ministry," in *Re-Union: The Necessary Requirements of the Church of Scotland. Scottish Church Society Conferences. Fourth Series,* 49-57. Edinburgh: L Gardner Hitt.

Leith Joh H 1973. *Assembly at Westminster. Reformed Theology in the Making.* Atlanta: John Knox Press.

Lightfoot John. *The Whole Works of the Rev. John Lightfoot, D.D., Master of Catharine Hall, Cambridge, Volume XIII. Containing the Journal of the Proceedings of the Assembly of Divines: From January 1, 1643, to 31 December 1644. And Letters to and from Dr Lightfoot.* Edited by John Rogers Pitman, 1824. London: J.F. Dove.

Lindsay Prof, CG M'Crie, W Blair, W Landels amd NL Walker 1888. *Religous Life in Scotland; From the Reformation to the Present Day.* London: T. Nelson and Sons.

Lorimer John G 1842a. *The Eldership of the Church of Scotland.* (2nd Edition) Glasgow: William Collins.

Lorimer John G 1842b. *The Deaconship. A Treatise on the Office of the Deacon with suggestions for its Revival.* Edinburgh: John Johnstone.

M'Crie Thomas 1856. *Life of Andrew Melville.* Edinburgh: Blackwood and Sons. A new edition by his son.

McEwen JS 1982. "How the Westminster Confession came to be Written," in *The Westminster Confession of Faith in the Church Today,* edited by Alasdair IC Heron. Edinburgh: The Saint Andrew Press.

MacInnes John 1966. "The Historical Background of the Westeminster Confession," in *Records of the Scottish Church History Society,* xv57-75. Edinburgh.

Machin Ian 1983. "Voluntaryism and Reunion, 1874-1929," in *Church, Politics and Society. Scotland 1408-1929,* 85-96. Edited by Norman MacDougall, Edinburgh: John Donald Publishers Ltd.

Maciver IF 1980. "The Evangelical Party and the Eldership in the General Assemblies, 1820-1843," in *Records of the Scottish Church History Society*, xx:1-14. Edinburgh.

MacGregor Geddes 1959. *Corpus Christi. The Nature of the Church according to the Reformed Tradition.* London: Macmillan and CO LTD.

Macgregor Janet G 1926. *The Scottish Presbyterian Polity. A Study of its Origins in the Sixteenth Century.* Edinburgh: Oliver and Boyd.

M'Kerrow John 1841. *History of the Secession Church. Revised and Enlarged.* Glasgow:

M'Kerrow John 1846. *The Office of the Ruling Elder in the Christian Church: Its Divine Authority, Duties and Responsibilities.* Edinburgh: William Oliphant and Sons.

Mackie JD 1966. *A History of the Church of Scotland.* Edited by Gordon Donaldson. New York. New York: Frederick A. Praeger.

McMahon George IR 1966: "The Scottish Courts of High Commission 1610-38," in *Records of the Scottish Church History Society*, xv:193-209.

McNeill John T 1943. "The Doctrine of the Ministry in Reformed Theology," in *Church History*, xii:77-97.

Mcleod John 1974. *Scottish Theology In Relation to Church History.* Edinburgh: The Knox Press. (1st Edition 1943).

MacPhail WM 1908. *The Presbyterian Church. A Brief Account of its Doctrine, Worship, and Polity.* London: Hodder and Stoughton.

Macpherson John [1883]. *Presbyterianism.* Edinburgh: T&T Clark.

Macpherson John 1903. *The Doctrine of the Church in Scottish Theology. The Sixth Series of the Chalmers Lectures.* Edited by C.G. M'Crie. Edinburgh: Macniven and Wallace.

Mair William 1880. *The Elders' Formula in the Church of Scotland. A Letter to the Right Honourable Lord Polwarth.* Edinburgh: William Blackwood and Sons.

Mair W (ed) 1913. *The Confession of Faith, the Larger Catechism, the Shorter Catechism, The Directory for Publick Worship, the Form of Presbyterial Church-Government.* Edinburgh, William Blackwood.

Makey Walter 1979. *The Church of the Covenant, 1637-1651. Revolution and Social Change in Scotland.* Edinburgh: John Donald Publishers Ltd.

Makey Walter 1983. "Presbyterian and Canterburian in the Scottish Revolution," in *Church, Politics and Society. Scotland 1408-1929*, 151-166. Edited by Norman MacDougall. Edinburgh: John Donald Publishers Ltd.

Matthew Steward and Ken Lawson 1989. *Caring for God's People. A Handbook for Elders and Ministers on Pastoral Care.* Edinburgh: The Saint Andrew Press.

Mechie Stewart 1963a. "Education for the Ministry in Scotland since the Reformation," in *Records of the Scottish Church History Society*, xiv:115-133. Glasgow.

Mechie Stewart 1963b. "Education for the Ministry in Scotland since the Reformation," in *Records of the Scottish Church History Society,* xiv:161-178. Glasgow.

Mechie Steward 1967. "The Theological Climate in the Early Eighteenth Century Scotland," in *Reformation and Revolution. Essays Presented to the Very Reverend Principal Emeritus Hugh Watt, D.D., D.Litt., on the Sixtieth Anniversary of his Ordination.* Edited by Duncan Shaw, Edinburgh: The Saint Andrew Press.

Milner BJ 1970. *Calvin's Doctrine of the Church.* Leiden: Brill.

Milligan William 1893. *Scottish Church Society, Some Account of its Aims.* Edinburgh: J. Gardner Hitt.

Milroy A 1890. "The Doctrine of the Church of Scotland," in Story, RB (ed) *The Church of Scotland, Past and Present. Its history, its relation to the law and the state, its doctrine, ritual, discipline, and patrimony. Volume IV.* London: William Mackenzie.

Mitchell Alex. F and John Struthers (eds) 1874. *Minutes of the Sessions of the Westminster Assembly of Divines, while engaged in preparing their Directory for Church Government Confession of Faith, and Catechism.* Edinburgh: William Blackwood and Sons.

Mitchell Alexander F 1883. *The Westminster Assembly. Its History and Standards.* Being the Baird Lecture for 1882. London: James Nisbet & Co.

Mitchell AF 1900. *The Scottish Reformation.* Edited by D. Hay Fleming. Edinburgh: William Blackwood and Sons.

Moncrieff H Wellwood (Convernor) 1886. *The Practice of the Free Church of Scotland in her Several Courts.* Fourth Edition. Revised. Edinburgh: Macniven and Wallace.

Noll Mark A (ed) 1983. *The Princeton Theology 1812-1921. Scripture, Science, and Theological Method from Archibald Alexander to Benjamin Breckinridge Warfield.* Grand Rapids: Baker Book House.

Ogilvie James D 1926. "Church Union in 1641," in *Records of the Scottish Church History Society,* i:143-160. Edinburgh.

Panel on Doctrine 1971. *The Office of Elder in the Church of Scotland.* Edinburgh: The Saint Andrew Press. (First printed 1964).

Parson Gerald (ed) 1988. *Religion in Victorian Britain. Vol 1. Traditions.* Manchester: Manchester University Press.

Paul Robert S 1985. *The Assembly of the Lord. Politics and Religion in the Westminister Assembly and the "Grand Debate."* Edinburgh: T&T Clark.

[Peterkin A] 1829. *A Compendium of the Laws of the Church of Scotland. Part First.* Edinburgh, Robert Buchanan.

Peterkin A 1831 *A Compendium of the Laws of the Church of Scotland. Part Second.* Edinburgh, Robert Buchanan.

Peterkin Alexander (ed) 1838. *Records of the Kirk of Scotland, containing the Acts and Proceedings of the General Assemblies of the Church of Scotland, from the year 1638 Downwards. Vol. 1.* Edinburgh.

Peterkin A (ed) 1839. *The Booke of the Universall Kirk of Scotland*, one volume edition. Edinburgh.

Pont AD 1981. *Die Historiese Agtergronde van ons Kerklike Reg.* Kaapstad: HAUM Uitgewery.

Proceedings of the General Assembly of the Free Church of Scotland, 1843. Edinburgh: James Greig & Son.

Proceedings of the Synod of the United Presbyterian Church, 1848-1856. 1856. Edinburgh: James Hogg.

Pryde George S 1962. *Scotland from 1603 to the Present Day. A New History of Scotland. Vol. II.* London: Thomas Nelson and Sons Ltd.

Reid JKS 1955. "The Biblical Doctrine of the Ministry," in *Scottish Journal of Theology Occasional Papers,* 4:1-47. Edinburgh: Oliver and Boyd Ltd.

Reid JKS 1966. "Diakonia in the Thought of Calvin," in *Service in Christ. Essay in Honour of Karl Barth on his 80th Birthday.* Edited by James McCord and THL Parker, 110-109. London. Epworth Press.

Reid W Stanford 1982. *Trumpeter of God. A Biography of John Knox.* Grand Rapids: Baker Book House.

Renwick AM 1960. *The Story of the Scottish Reformation.* Second edition. London: Inter-Varsity Fellowship.

Reports to the General Assembly of the Church of Scotland, 1931-94. Church of Scotland, Edinburgh.

Rogers Jack Bartlett 1966. *Scripture in the Westminster Confession. A Problem of Historical Interpretation for American Presbyterians.* Kampen: Kok.

Ross Kenneth R 1988. *Church and Creed in Scotland. The Free Church Case 1900-1904 and its Origins.* Edinburgh: Rutherford House Books.

Rossouw PJ (ed) 1985. *Gereformeerde Ampsbediening.* Goodwood: N.G.K.B.

Row, John 1842. *The History of the Kirk of Scotland. From 1558 to 1637. With a Continuation to July 1639 by his son, John Row.* Edited by David Laing. Edinburgh: Printed for the Wodrow Society.

Rules and Forms of the Procedure of the United Presbyterian Church, 1883. Edinburgh: United Presbyterian College Buildings.

Rules and Forms of the Procedure of the United Presbyterian Church, 1885. Edinburgh: United Presbyterian College Buildings.

Rutherford Samuel 1644. *The Due Right of Presbyteries or, A peacable Plea for the Government of the Church of Scotland.* London: E. Griffin.

Rutherford Samuel 1646. *The Divine Right of Church-Government and Excommunication: or A Peacable Dispute for the perfection of the holy*

Scripture in point of ceremonies and Church Government in which the Removal of the Service-Book is justified. Published by authority.London.

Scottish Church Society Conferences, 1895. *Divine life in the Church. An Affirmation of the Doctrine of Holy Baptism. With contributions relating to the Scottish Church, her History, Work, and Present need.* Edinburgh: H. Gardner Hitt.

Scottish Church Society, 1929. *Presbyterian Orders. Occasional Papers IV.* Edinburgh: Andrew Elliot. First printed 1926.

Shaw Duncan 1964. *The General Assemblies of the Church of Scotland, 1560-1600. Their Origins and Development.* Edinburgh: The Saint Andrew Press.

Shaw Duncan 1969. "The Inauguration of Ministers in Scotland," in *Records of the Scottish Church History Society,* xvi::35-62. Glasgow.

Sher Richard and Alexander Murdoch 1983. "Patronage and Party in the Church of Scotland, 1750-1800," *in Church, Politics and Society. Scotland 1408-1929.* Edited by Norman MacDougall, 197-220. Edinburgh: John Donald Publishers Ltd.

Simpson Martin A 1983. "The Hampton Court Conference, January 1604," in *Records of the Scottish Church History Society,* xxi:27-41. Edinburgh.

Speelman HA 1994. *Calvijn en de Zelfstandigheid van de Kerk.* Kampen: Uitgeverij Kok.

Spoelstra B 1991. "Presbiteriale Kerkregering en Presbyterianisme," in *Nederduitse Gereformeerde Teologies Tydskrif,* 32:1991:57-67.

Sprott GW 1873. *A Valid Ordination Essential to the Christian Ministry, and the Exclusive Right of Presbyteries to Ordain:* A Sermon preached at the opening of the Synod of Aberdeen, 8 April 1873. Aberdeen: John Rae Smith. Reprinted 1896.

Sprott GW 1882. *Worship and Offices of the Church of Scotland.* Edinburgh: William Blackwood and Sons.

Sprott GW 1877. *The Church Principles of the Reformation.* A Sermon preached before the Synod of Lothian and Tweeddale. Edinburgh: William Blackwood and Sons.

Sprott GW 1895. "Neglected Provisions and Remediable Defects in the Presbyterian Organisation, and its better adoption to existing needs," *in Scottish Church Society Conferences, Second Series: Vol. II: The Divine Life in the Church. An Affirmation of the Doctrine of Holy Baptism with contributions relating to the Scottish Church, her History, Work, and Present need,* 59-66. Edinburgh: J Gardner Hitt.

Steward Kenneth James 1984. *Unity and Diversity in English and Scottish Reformation.* A thesis presented to the University of Waterloo in fulfilment of the thesis requirements for the degree of Masters in Philosophy in History. Waterloo.

Story Robert Herbert 1897. *The Apostolic Ministry in the Scottish Church.* The Baird Lectures for 1897. Edinburgh: William Blackwood and Sons.
Story RB (ed) 1890. *The Church of Scotland, Past and Present. Its history, its relation to the law and the state, its doctrine, ritual, discipline, and patrimony. Five Volumes.* London: William Mackenzie.
Struthers Gavin 1843. *The History of the Rise, Progress and Principles of the Relief Church.* Glasgow.
The Church Law Society 1843. *Acts of the General Assembly of the Church of Scotland, 1638-1842.* Edinburgh. The Edinburgh Printing and Publishing Company.
The Practice of the Free Church of Scotland in her Several Courts. 1886. Edinburgh: Macniven and Wallace.
The Presbyterian Review and Religious Journal. November 1834-May 1835. Vol. VI:28-44; 161-177. Edinburgh, Waugh and Innes.
Torrance TF 1958. "Consecration and Ordination," in *Scottish Journal of Theology,* 11:225-252.
Torrance TF 1966. "Service in Christ," in *Service in Christ. Essay in Honour of Karl Barth on his 80th Birthday.* Edited by James McCord and THL Parker. London: Epworth Press, 1-16. Edinburgh: Scottish Academy Press.
Torrance TF 1984. "The Eldership in the Reformed Church," in *Scottish Journal of Theology.* 37:503-518.
Trevor-Roper Hugh 1987. *Catholics, Anglicans and Puritans.* London: Fontana Press.
Trimp C 1982. *Ministerium. Een introductie in de reformatoriesche leer van het ambt.* Groningen: Uitgeverij De Vuurbaak.
Van Ginkel A 1975. *De Ouderling. Oorsprong en Ontwikkeling van het Ambt van Ouderling en de Functie daarvan in de Gereformeerde Kerk de Nederlande in de 16e en 17e eeuw.* Amsterdam: Ton Bolland.
Van Harten PH 1986. *De Prediking van Ebenezer en Ralph Erskine. Evangelieverkondiging in het Spanningsveld van Verkiezing en Belofte.* s'Gravenhage: Uitgeverij Boekencentrum BV.
Van Itterzon GP 1974.*Het kerklijk ambt in geding.* Kampen: JH Kok.
Van't Spijker W and LC van Drimmelen (eds) [1988]. *Inleiding tot de Studie van het Kerkrecht.* Kampen: JH Kok.
Van't Spijker W, W Balke, K Exalto, L van Driel 1990. *De Kerk. Wezen, weg en werk van de Kerk naar reformatorische opvatting.* Kampen: Uitgeverij de Groot Goudriaan.
Walker David 1983. "Thomas Goodwin and the Debate on Church Government," *Journal of Ecclesiastical History,* 34:85-99. Cambridge: University Press.
Walker GMS 1955. "Scottish Ministerial Orders," in *Scottish Journal of Theology,* vol. 8:238-254. London: Oliver & Boyd Ltd.

Wallace William A 1895."The Development or Right lines of lay work in the Church - that of men," in *Scottish Church Society Conferences, Second Series: Vol. II: The Divine Life in the Church. An Affirmation of the Doctrine of Baptism with contributions relating to The Scottish Church, her History, Work, and Present need,* 113-122. Edinburgh: J. Gardner Hitt.

Wells David F (ed) 1989. *The Princeton Theology. Reformed Theology in America.* Grand Rapids: Baker Book House.

Werner Gn 1991. *De Schotse Kerkgeschiedenis.* Barneveld: Uitgeverij De Vuurbaak.

Wilkie George D 1961. *The Eldership Today.* 3rd Edition. Glasgow: An Iona Community Pamphlet. (First Edition 1958).

Withrington Donald J 1972: "Non-Church-Going, c.1750-c.1850: A Preliminary Study," in *Records of the Scottish Church History Society,* xvii:99-113. Edinburgh.

Wright Alexander 1895. *The Presbyterian Church. Its Worship, Functions, and Ministerial Orders.* Edinburgh: Oliphant Anderson & Ferreir.

Wotherspoon HJ 1909. "Adequate Security for the Continuance of the Ministry," in *Re-Union: The Necessary Requirements of the Church of Scotland.* Scottish Church Society Conferences. Fourth Series, 17-48. Edinburgh: J. Gardner Hitt.

Wotherspoon HJ and JM Kirkpatrick [1920]. *A Manual of Church Doctrine.* London: Hodder and Stoughton.

Wotherspoon HJ and JM Kirkpatrick 1960. *A Manual of Church Doctrine.* Second Edition Revised and enlarged by TF Torrance and RS Wright. London: Oxford University Press.